M000282404

GOD CRUCIFIED

GOD CRUCIFIED

Monotheism and Christology in the New Testament

Richard Bauckham

William B. Eerdmans Publishing Company
Grand Rapids, Michigan / Cambridge, U. K.

First published 1998 in Great Britain by
Paternoster Press
P.O. Box 300, Carlisle, Cumbria, CA3 0QS, U.K.

This edition published 1999 in the United States by
Wm. B. Eerdmans Publishing Co.
2140 Oak Industrial Drive N.E., Grand Rapids, Michigan 49505 /
P.O. Box 163, Cambridge CB3 9PU U.K.
www.eerdmans.com

Printed in the United States of America

12 11 10 09 08 07 10 9 8 7 6 5 4

Library of Congress Cataloging-in-Publication Data

ISBN 978-0-8028-4642-6 (pbk.: alk. paper)

Contents

Preface

This book is a version of the 1996 Didsbury Lectures, which I gave in October 1996 at the British Isles Nazarene College in Didsbury, Manchester. I have lightly revised the text of the lectures and added footnotes. There were four lectures, but I have combined the third and fourth into one chapter since the argument ran continuously through them.

The book contains a concise version of an argument which I shall publish in much fuller form in a book still in progress, provisionally entitled 'Jesus and the Identity of God: Jewish Monotheism and New Testament Christology'. In both books I present a new proposal for understanding New Testament Christology in its Jewish context. With current scholarly discussion about the nature of Jewish monotheism in the Second Temple period and attempts to find Jewish precedents for early Christology as my starting-points, I argue that recent trends to find a model for Christology in semi-divine intermediary figures in early Judaism are largely mistaken. Working with the key category of the identity of the God of Israel – which appropriately focuses on who God is rather than what divinity is – I show that early Judaism had clear and consistent ways of characterizing the unique identity of the one God and thus distinguishing the one God absolutely from all other reality. When New Testament Christology is read with this Jewish theological context in mind, it becomes clear that, from the earliest post-Easter beginnings of Christology onwards, early Christians included Jesus, precisely and unambiguously, within the unique identity of the one God of Israel. They did so by including Jesus in the unique, defining characteristics by which Jewish monotheism identified God as unique. They did not have to break with Jewish monotheism in order to do this, since monotheism, as Second Temple Judaism understood it, was structurally open to the development of the christological monotheism that we find in the New Testament texts.

The earliest Christology was already the highest Christology. I call it a Christology of divine identity, proposing this as a way to move beyond the standard distinction between 'functional' and 'ontic' Christology, a distinction which does not correspond to early Jewish thinking about God and has therefore seriously distorted our understanding of New Testament Christology. When we think in terms of divine identity, rather than divine essence or nature, which are not the primary categories for Jewish theology, we can see that the so-called divine functions which Jesus exercises are intrinsic to who God is. This Christology of divine identity is not a mere stage on the way to the patristic development of ontological Christology in the context of a trinitarian theology. It is already a fully divine Christology, maintaining that Jesus Christ is intrinsic to the unique and eternal identity of God. The Fathers did not develop it so much as transpose it into a conceptual framework constructed more in terms of the Greek philosophical categories of essence and nature.

The inclusion of Jesus in the unique divine identity had implications not only for who Jesus is but also for who God is. This forms the second half of the argument I pursue in this book and will develop more fully in the longer work. When it was taken seriously, as it was in the major forms of New Testament theology, that not only the pre-existent and the exalted Jesus but also the earthly, suffering, humiliated and crucified Jesus belong to the unique identity of God, then it had to be said that Jesus reveals the divine identity – who God truly is – in humiliation as well as exaltation, and in the connexion of the two. God's own identity is revealed in Jesus, his life and his cross, just as truly as in his exaltation, in a way that is fully continuous and consistent with the Old Testament and Jewish understanding of God, but is also novel and surprising. While the Fathers successfully appropriated, in their own way in Nicene theology, the New Testament's inclusion of Jesus in the identity of God, they were less successful in appropriating this corollary, the revelation of the divine identity in Jesus' human life and passion. To see justice done to this aspect of New Testament Christology we have to turn to the kind of theology of the cross which Martin Luther adumbrated and which has come into its own in the twentieth century.

It will be seen that my thesis is not only a historical account of the background, origins and nature of New Testament Christology, but is also highly significant for our evaluation of the church's christological tradition and for contemporary constructive theology. In the present book I am able only to indicate this briefly at the end. It will be much more developed in my longer treatment.

In the present concise version of my argument, not only have I been unable to develop some major aspects of the argument, I have also not been able to provide the detailed study of the texts and the thorough interaction with other interpretations of Jewish monotheism, New Testament Christology, and the key early Jewish and early Christian texts, that will be needed to establish my arguments adequately in the context of current scholarly discussion. This has to await the fuller study. But many readers will no doubt find the present form of my argument, uncluttered by too much exegetical detail and scholarly apparatus, much easier to appreciate and to assimilate. I am very glad of this opportunity to publish my work in this form, which is not so much a 'popular' as a concise version, in which the wood is not lost among the trees, and the main contours of my central argument are clearly visible.

It was an honour to join what is now a very distinguished succession of Didsbury lecturers and a pleasure to be back in Manchester, where I taught at the University for fifteen years until 1992, knew the Nazarene College, and even attended previous Didsbury Lectures. I am most grateful to the College and especially to its Dean, Dr Kent Brower, for inviting me to lecture, as well as for entertaining me generously during my stay. Staff, students and members of the public who attended the lectures helped to make it a stimulating as well as enjoyable experience. I must also thank my St Andrews colleague Trevor

Hart for a conversation as a direct result of which I conceived the idea for these lectures, out of which also rapidly grew the larger project of which they are the first fruits. The thinking which is crystallized here has, without having this end consciously in view, developed over many years of study of early Judaism, the New Testament, and historical and contemporary Christology. It is therefore indebted to many books and many people, including many students who took my courses on Christology. I cannot acknowledge all these debts other than in this general way, but nor can I contemplate this completed book without being gratefully aware of them.

Richard Bauckham
St Mary's College
St Andrews
May 1998

Chapter One

Understanding Early Jewish Monotheism

Early Jewish monotheism and New Testament Christology in recent discussion

The key question this book addresses is the relationship between Jewish monotheism – the Jewish monotheism of the Second Temple period which was the context of Christian origins – and New Testament Christology. Recent discussion of New Testament Christology makes it abundantly clear that this relationship is central to the debate about the character and development of early Christology. How New Testament authors understand the relationship of Jesus to God, how far they attribute some kind of divinity to Jesus, what kind of divinity it is that they attribute to him – such questions are deeply involved with questions about the way Second Temple Judaism understood the uniqueness of God. Of course, assumptions about the character of Jewish monotheism have always informed modern scholarly interpretation of New Testament Christology. What is relatively new in recent discussion is that there is now a significant debate in progress about the nature of Jewish monotheism in this period.[1] Interestingly, most participants in this debate are concerned precisely with the way in which the view of Jewish monotheism they argue affects the interpretation of New Testament Christology. A range of different views as to the nature of Second Temple Jewish monotheism (or, indeed, as

---

1 See the valuable survey in L. W. Hurtado, 'What Do We Mean by "First-Century Jewish Monotheism"?', *SBLSP* 1993, 348–354.

to whether the term 'monotheism' is appropriate at all) correlate with a similar range of views as to the process by which Jesus came to be regarded as divine and the sense in which he was considered divine in the Christian churches of the New Testament period.

Simplifying somewhat the range of views for the sake of illustration, one can identify two main approaches. There is, first, the view that Second Temple Judaism was characterized by a 'strict' monotheism that made it impossible to attribute real divinity to any figure other than the one God. From this view of Jewish monotheism, some argue that Jesus cannot have been treated as really divine within a Jewish monotheistic context, so that only a radical break with Jewish monotheism could make the attribution of real divinity to Jesus possible.[2] Given the obviously very Jewish character of earliest Christianity, this approach tends to interpret the evidence in such a way as to minimize the extent to which anything like really divine Christology can be found within the New Testament texts.

Secondly, there are revisionist views of Second Temple Judaism which in one way or another deny its strictly monotheistic character. Such views usually focus on various kinds of intermediary figures – principal angels, exalted humans, personified divine attributes or functions – who are understood to occupy a subordinate divine or semi-divine status, so that the distinction between the one God and all other reality was by no means absolute in the Judaism of this period, it is claimed. Such views are closely related to a search for Jewish precedents and parallels for early Christian Christology. Such scholars often recognize both that many New Testament texts really do treat Jesus as in some way divine, and also that these texts are clearly working within a fundamentally Jewish conceptual context. The attempt to understand how such high Christology could develop within a Jewish movement focuses

---

2 A. E. Harvey, *Jesus and the Constraints of History* (London: Duckworth, 1982) chapter 7; P. M. Casey, *From Jewish Prophet to Gentile God* (Cambridge: J. Clarke; Louisville: Westminster/John Knox, 1991); idem, 'The Deification of Jesus', *SBLSP* 1994, 697–714.

then on the intermediary figures of Second Temple Judaism who in some way participate in divinity. Such figures provide, as it were, an already existing Jewish category into which early Christian estimations of Jesus' exalted status could fit. Because Jewish monotheism was not strict but flexible, and the boundary between the one God and all other reality relatively blurred by the interest in intermediary figures, the highest New Testament Christology can be understood as an intelligibly Jewish development.[3]

The view I shall argue in the first two chapters of this book differs from both these approaches. In common with the first view, I shall argue that the monotheism of Second Temple Judaism was indeed 'strict'. I shall argue that most Jews in this period were highly self-consciously monotheistic and had certain very familiar and well-defined ideas as to how the uniqueness of the one God should be understood. In other words, they drew the line of distinction between the one God and all other reality clearly, and were in the habit of distinguishing God from all other reality by means of certain clearly articulated criteria. So-called intermediary figures were not ambiguous semi-divinities straddling the boundary

[3] C. Rowland, *The Open Heaven* (London: SPCK, 1982) 94–113; A. Chester, 'Jewish Messianic Expectations and Mediatorial Figures and Pauline Christology', in M. Hengel and U. Heckel ed., *Paulus und antike Judentum* (WUNT 58; Tübingen: Mohr [Siebeck], 1991) 17–89; M. Barker, *The Great Angel: A Study of Israel's Second God* (London: SPCK, 1992); C. A. Gieschen, *Angelomorphic Christology* (AGJU 42; Leiden: Brill, 1998). For a variety of related views which stress the importance of Jewish intermediary figures for the development of Christology, see also: M. Hengel, *The Son of God* (tr. J. Bowden; London: SCM Press, 1976); J. D. G. Dunn, *Christology in the Making* (London: SCM Press, 1980); idem, 'Was Christianity a Monotheistic Faith from the Beginning?', *SJT* 35 (1982) 303–336; idem, 'The Making of Christology: – Evolution or Unfolding?', in J. B. Green and M. Turner ed., *Jesus of Nazareth: Lord and Christ* (I. H. Marshall FS; Grand Rapids: Eerdmans; Carlisle: Paternoster, 1994) 437–452; L. W. Hurtado, *One God, One Lord: Early Christian Devotion and Ancient Jewish Monotheism* (Philadelphia: Fortress, 1988).

between God and creation. Some were understood as aspects of the one God's own unique reality. Most were regarded as unambiguously creatures, exalted servants of God whom the literature often takes pains to distinguish clearly from the truly divine reality of the one and only God. Therefore, differing from the second view, I do not think such Jewish intermediary figures are of any decisive importance for the study of early Christology. While not denying that some of them have some relevance, I think the intensive interest in them as the key to understanding the Jewishness of early Christology has been misleading. The real continuity between Jewish monotheism and New Testament Christology is not to be found in intermediary figures.

Instead, I shall argue that high Christology was possible within a Jewish monotheistic context, not by applying to Jesus a Jewish category of semi-divine intermediary status, but by identifying Jesus directly with the one God of Israel, including Jesus in the unique identity of this one God. Jewish monotheism clearly distinguished the one God and all other reality, but the ways in which it distinguished the one God from all else did not prevent the early Christians including Jesus in this unique divine identity. While this was a radically novel development, almost unprecedented in Jewish theology, the character of Jewish monotheism was such that this development did not require any repudiation of the ways in which Jewish monotheism understood the uniqueness of God. What has been lacking in the whole discussion of this issue has been an adequate understanding of the ways in which Second Temple Judaism understood the uniqueness of God. By acquiring such an understanding, we shall be able to see that what the New Testament texts in general do is take up the well-known Jewish monotheistic ways of distinguishing the one God from all other reality and use these precisely as ways of including Jesus in the unique identity of the one God as commonly understood in Second Temple Judaism.

Before proceeding to argue this view, I wish to make two brief general criticisms of the way the discussions of Jewish monotheism and early Christology have tended to proceed. One is that the fundamentally important question – what, in the Jewish understanding of God, really counts as 'divine' – is rarely faced with clarity. In the discussion of whether Jewish monotheism was more or less strict or flexible, and in the discussion of the status of so-called intermediary figures, scholars tend to apply a variety of unexamined criteria for drawing the boundary between God and what is not God, or the divine and the non-divine.[4] Consequently it is also unclear what the attribution of divinity to Jesus in early Christology would really imply. Some (not all) scholars who seek Jewish precedent for early Christology in allegedly semi-divine or subordinately divine Jewish intermediary figures seem to think that this supports an interpretation of New Testament Christology favourable to later christological orthodoxy, the confession of the true divinity of Jesus Christ. In fact, such arguments often produce something much more like an Arian Christ, a demi-god who is neither truly divine nor truly human. The whole discussion of Jewish monotheism and early Christology urgently requires clarification of the way Jewish monotheism understood the uniqueness of God and drew the distinction between God and what is not God.

Secondly, assessment of the evidence for the character of Second Temple Jewish monotheism has, in my view, been distorted by concentration on the so-called intermediary figures in the belief that these constitute the parts of the evidence that will be most illuminating for understanding early Christology. Much of the clear evidence for the ways in which Second Temple Judaism understood the uniqueness of God has been neglected in favour of a small amount of highly debatable evidence. Intermediary figures who may or may not participate in divinity are by no means characteristic of the literature of Second Temple Judaism. They should not be the focus of a study of Second Temple Jewish monotheism. Rather we should proceed by studying the broader evidence of the way the uniqueness of God was understood, and then consider the intermediary figures in the context of this broader evidence.

---

4 A good start towards clarity in discussion is the list of 'criteria of divinity' in Gieschen, *Angelomorphic Christology*, 31–33, though I would reduce and modify his list in some respects.

Second Temple Judaism as self-consciously monotheistic

There is every reason to suppose that observant Jews of the late Second Temple period were highly self-conscious monotheists, in the sense that they saw their worship of and obedience to the one and only God, the God of Israel, as defining their distinctive religious way in the pluralistic religious environment of their time. The best evidence is their use of two key monotheistic passages of Scripture. One was the *Shema'*, the passage in Deuteronomy (6:4–6) which begins, 'Hear, O Israel: YHWH our God, YHWH is one', and continues with the requirement of total devotion to this one God: 'You shall love YHWH your God with all your heart, and with all your soul, and with all your might'. The other was the Decalogue, whose first two commandments forbid Israelites to have or to worship any gods but YHWH (Exod. 20:2–6; Deut. 5:6–10). Both passages were clearly understood in this period as asserting the absolute uniqueness of YHWH as the one and only God. The first, the *Shema'*, was recited twice daily, morning and evening, by all Jews who were concerned to practise Torah faithfully, since it was believed that the Torah itself commanded such twice daily recitation of this passage. Moreover, there is evidence that in this period the passage recited included not only the *Shema'* itself but also the Decalogue. Observant Jews, therefore, were daily reminded of their allegiance to the one God alone. Their self-conscious monotheism was not merely an intellectual belief about God, but a unity of belief and praxis, involving the exclusive worship of this one God and exclusive obedience to this one God. Monolatry (the worship of only the one God) as the corollary of monotheism (belief in only the one God) is an important aspect of Jewish monotheism to which we shall return.

The unique identity of God in Jewish monotheism

This kind of practical monotheism, requiring a whole pattern of daily life and cultic worship formed by exclusive allegiance to the one God, presupposes a god who is in some way significantly identifiable. The God who requires what the God of Israel requires cannot be merely the philosophical abstraction to which the intellectual currents of contemporary Greek thought aspired. Jews in some sense knew who their God was. The God of Israel had a unique identity. The concept which will be the central focus of the whole argument of this book is that of the identity of God.[5] Since the biblical God has a name and a character, since this God acts, speaks, relates, can be addressed, and in some sense known, the analogy of human personal identity suggests itself as the category with which to synthesize the biblical and Jewish understanding of God. It is the analogy which is clearly at work in much of the literary portrayal of God in biblical and Jewish literature. In the narratives of Israel's history, for example, God acts as a character in the story, identifiable in ways similar to those in which human characters in the story are identifiable. He has

[5] For the notion of identity as I use it here, see H. W. Frei, *The Identity of Jesus Christ* (Philadelphia: Fortress Press, 1975); idem, 'Theological Reflections on the Accounts of Jesus' Death and Resurrection', in H. W. Frei, *Theology and Narrative: Selected Essays* (ed. G. Hunsinger and W. C. Placher; New York/Oxford: Oxford University Press, 1993) 45–93; D. Patrick, *The Rendering of God in the Old Testament* (Philadelphia: Fortress, 1981); R. W. Jenson, *The Triune Identity* (Philadelphia: Fortress, 1982); R. F. Thiemann, *Revelation and Theology: The Gospel as Narrated Promise* (Notre Dame, Indiana: University of Notre Dame Press, 1985) chapters 6–7; R. A. Krieg, *Story-Shaped Christology: Identifying Jesus Christ* (New York: Paulist Press, 1988) chapter 1; K. J. Vanhoozer, 'Does the Trinity Belong in a Theology of Religions? On Angling in the Rubicon and the "Identity" of God', in K. J. Vanhoozer ed., *The Trinity in a Pluralistic Age* (Grand Rapids: Eerdmans, 1997) 41–71. As Vanhoozer notes, ' "Identity" is, of course, susceptible of several meanings: numeric oneness, ontological sameness or permanence in time, and the personal identity of self-continuity' (47). The last is the meaning employed here. Reference to God's identity is by analogy with human personal identity, understood not as a mere ontological subject without characteristics, but as including both character and personal story (the latter entailing relationships). These are the ways in which we commonly specify 'who someone is'.

a personal identity, as Abraham and David do. This is not to say that the human analogy is adequate. All biblical and Jewish literature, even those passages which on the surface seem naively anthropomorphic in their portrayal of God, are aware of the transcendence of God, such that language and concepts are stretched when applied to him. As we shall see, the identity of God, in the Jewish understanding, breaks out of the human analogy, but its starting-point is clearly the analogy of human personal identity.

The term 'identity' is mine, not that of the ancient literature, but I use it as a label for what I do find in the literature, which is not of course necessarily a notion precisely the same as modern ideas of personal identity, but is nevertheless clearly a concern with who God is. The value of the concept of divine identity appears partly if we contrast it with a concept of divine essence or nature. Identity concerns who God is; nature concerns what God is or what divinity is. Greek philosophy, in a way that was to influence the Christian theological tradition in the period after the New Testament, typically defined divine nature by means of a series of metaphysical attributes: ingenerateness, incorruptibility, immutability, and so on. My point is not that the biblical and Jewish tradition had no use at all for statements about divine nature. Some Jewish writers in the later Second Temple period consciously adopted some of the Greek metaphysical language.[6] But even in these writers the dominant conceptual framework of their understanding of God is not a definition of divine nature – what divinity is – but a notion of the divine identity, characterized primarily in ways other than metaphysical attributes. That God is eternal, for example – a claim essential to all Jewish thinking about God – is not so much a statement about what divine nature is, more an element in the unique divine identity, along with claims that God alone created all things and rules all things, that God is gracious and merciful and just, that God brought Israel out of Egypt and made Israel his own people and gave Israel his law at Sinai, and so on. If we wish to know in what Second Temple

[6] E.g. Josephus, *Ant.* 1.15, 19; 8.107; *C. Ap.* 2.167–168.

Judaism considered the uniqueness of the one God to consist, what distinguished God as unique from all other reality, including beings worshipped as gods by Gentiles, we must look not for a definition of divine nature, but for ways of characterizing the unique divine identity.

Characterizing the unique identity of God

For convenience I will distinguish two categories of identifying features of the God of Israel. There are those which identify God in his relationship to Israel and there are those which identify God in his relation to all reality. The categories are not, of course, unrelated, but the distinction will be helpful for my argument. To Israel, God has revealed and is known by his name YHWH, which was of great importance to Second Temple Jews because it names the unique identity of God. In addition to his name, God's identity is known to Israel from the recital of his acts in history and from the revelation of his character to Israel. Through much of the Hebrew Bible YHWH is identified as the God who brought Israel out of Egypt and by the remarkable events of the Exodus period created a people for himself (e.g. Exod. 20:2; Deut. 4:32–39; Isa. 43:15–17). In addition to identification of him by his activities, there is also a character description, given by God himself in his self-revelation to Moses: 'YHWH, YHWH, a God merciful and gracious, slow to anger, and abounding in steadfast love and faithfulness . . .' (Exod. 34:6 and constantly echoed elsewhere in the biblical and later Jewish literature[7]). The acts of God and the character description of God combine to indicate a consistent identity of the One who acts graciously towards his people and can be expected to do so. Through the consistency of his acts and character, the One called YHWH shows himself to be one and the same.

Alongside such identifications of God in his covenant relationship with Israel, there are also characterizations of his

[7] Num. 14:18; Neh. 9:17; Ps. 103:8; Joel 2:13; Jonah 4:2; Sir. 2:11; *Pr. Man.* 7; *4 Ezra* 7:132–140; *Jos. Asen.* 11:10; 1QH 11:29–30.

identity by reference to his unique relationship to the whole of reality: most especially, that he is Creator of all things and sovereign Ruler of all things. It is worth noting at this point (since it will be important to us in a later chapter) that the two categories of identifying features come together with special combined significance in Israel's eschatological expectation. In the future, when God will fulfil his promises to his own people, showing himself to be finally and definitively the gracious God they have known in their history from the Exodus onwards, God will at the same time demonstrate his deity to the nations, implementing his sovereignty as Creator and Ruler of all things in establishing his universal kingdom, making his name known universally, becoming known to all as the God Israel has known. The new Exodus of the future, especially as predicted in the prophecies we call Deutero-Isaiah (Isa. 40–55), will be an event of universal significance precisely because the God who brought Israel out of Egypt is also the Creator and Ruler of all things.

For the moment, however, we leave aside the first category of identifying features of God. They did not cease to be of central importance for the Jewish understanding of the identity of God, and we shall return to them in the last chapter. But we shall focus now on those ways of characterizing the unique divine identity which refer to God's relationship to the whole of reality. The reason for doing so is that in the literature of Second Temple Judaism these are the features of the divine identity on which Jews focused when they wished to identify God as unique. To our question, 'In what did Second Temple Judaism consider the uniqueness of the one God to consist? What distinguished God as unique from all other reality, including beings worshipped as gods by Gentiles?', the answer given again and again, in a wide variety of Second Temple Jewish literature, is that the only true God, YHWH, the God of Israel, is sole Creator of all things[8]

[8] Isa. 40:26, 28; 42:5; 44:24; 45:12, 18; 48:13; 51:16; Neh. 9:6; Hos. 13:4 LXX; 2 Macc. 1:24; Sir. 43:33; Bel 5; *Jub.* 12:3–5; *Sib. Or.* 3:20–35; 8:375–376; Frag. 1:5–6; Frag. 3; Frag. 5; *2 Enoch* 47:3–4; 66:4; *Apoc. Abr.* 7:10; *Pseudo-Sophocles*; *Jos. Asen.* 12:1–2; *T. Job* 2:4.

and sole Ruler of all things.[9] While these characteristics are by no means *sufficient* to identify God (since they say nothing, for example, about his goodness or his justice), they are the features which most readily distinguish God absolutely from all other reality. God alone created all things; all other things, including beings worshipped as gods by Gentiles, are created by him. God alone rules supreme over all things; all other things, including beings worshipped as gods by Gentiles, are subject to him. These ways of distinguishing God as unique formed a very easily intelligible way of defining the uniqueness of the God they worshipped that every Jew in every synagogue in the late Second Temple period would certainly have known. However diverse Judaism may have been in many other respects, this was common: only the God of Israel is worthy of worship because he is sole Creator of all things and sole Ruler of all things. Other beings who might otherwise be thought divine are by these criteria God's creatures and subjects.

The emphasis on God's uniqueness as Creator and sovereign Ruler of history occurs in the Hebrew Bible especially in the great divine assertions of God's unique deity in Deutero-Isaiah, where they are the basis of the expectation that God will demonstrate his unique deity to the ends of the earth in the future. We shall return frequently to Deutero-Isaiah in this book. Those chapters of Isaiah were, outside the Torah, the most important sources of Second Temple Jewish monotheism. Again and again, Deutero-Isaiah's expressions of God's uniqueness are echoed in later Jewish literature. The Lord is God, and there is no god besides him,[10] who created all things and reigns

---

9 Dan. 4:34–35; Bel 5; Add. Est. 13:9–11; 16:18, 21; 3 Macc. 2:2–3; 6:2; Wis. 12:13; Sir. 18:1–3; *Sib. Or.* 3:10, 19; Frag. 1:7, 15, 17, 35; *1 Enoch* 9:5; 84:3; 2 *Enoch* 33:7; 2 *Bar.* 54:13; Josephus, *Ant.* 1:155–156.

10 This monotheistic formula appears very frequently in the Hebrew Bible and Second Temple Jewish literature: Deut. 4:35, 39; 32:39; 1 Sam. 2:2; 2 Sam. 7:22; Isa. 43:11; 44:6; 45:5, 6, 14, 18, 21, 22; 46:9; Hos. 13:4; Joel 2:27; Wis. 12:13; Jdt. 8:20; 9:14; Bel 41; Sir. 24:24; 36:5; 4Q504 [4QDibHam^{a}] 5:9; 1Q35 1:6; Bar. 3:36; *2 Enoch* 33:8; 36:1; 47:3; *Sib. Or.* 3:629, 760; 8:377; *T. Abr.* A8:7; *Orphica* 16; Philo, *Leg. All.* 3.4, 82.

supreme over all things: these themes run from Deutero-Isaiah right through the whole literature of Second Temple Judaism.

Both these aspects of God's unique identity are aspects of his absolute supremacy over all things, and are frequently connected very closely in the literature. There is one respect, however, which will be important for the argument of these lectures, in which they differ. In creation God acted alone: 'I . . . alone stretched out the heavens [and] . . . by myself spread out the earth' (Isa. 44:24). As the only eternal one (another frequent and related characterization of God in the Second Temple period[11]), God alone brought all other beings into existence. God had no helper, assistant or servant to assist or to implement his work of creation.[12] God alone created, and no one else had any part in this activity. This is axiomatic for Second Temple Judaism.

In his sovereignty over the universe and history, however, God, of course, employs servants, especially the myriads of angels. Here the dominant image is of God as the great emperor ruling the cosmos as his kingdom, and employing, like a human emperor, vast numbers of servants who do his will throughout his empire. In this sense the activity of others who implement God's sovereignty is important, but the Jewish concern to emphasize the uniqueness of God's total sovereignty means that angels are invariably portrayed as servants whose role is simply to carry out the will of God in total obedience. They do not share in his rule; they serve. While God sits on his throne, the angels, even the greatest, stand, in the posture of servants, awaiting his command to serve.[13] The

---

[11] Tob. 13:1; Sir. 18:1; 2 Macc. 1:25; *T. Mos.* 10:7; *1 Enoch* 5:1.

[12] Isa. 44:24; *2 Enoch* 33:4; *4 Ezra* 3:4; Josephus, *C. Ap.* 2.192. Even Philo's exegesis of Gen. 1:26 (*De Opif. Mundi* 72–75; *De Conf. Ling.* 179) is only a minor qualification of this denial: he insists that God acted alone in the creation of all things except humanity, and holds that the plural in Gen. 1:26 involves subordinate co-workers of God so that, while good human actions may be attributed to God as their source, sins may not.

[13] Dan. 7:10; Tob. 12:15; 4Q530 2.18; *1 Enoch* 14:22; 39:12; 40:1; 47:3; 60:2; *2 Enoch* 21:1; *Qu. Ezra* A26, 30; *2 Bar.* 21:6; 48:10; *4 Ezra* 8:21; *T. Abr.* A7:11; 8:1–4; 9:7–8; *T. Adam* 2:9.

supremacy of God is frequently depicted in the evidently powerful imagery of height. God's great throne, from which he rules the whole cosmos, is situated in the heaven of heavens, exalted high over all the many heavenly realms[14] in which his glorious angelic servants sing his praise and do his will. Even the most exalted angels, God's ministers of state, cannot approach the high and lofty throne[15] which towers above them at the summit of the universe.

So the participation of other beings in God's unique supremacy over all things is ruled out, in the case of creation, by excluding them from any role at all, and, in sovereignty over the cosmos, by placing them in strict subordination as servants, excluding any possibility of interpreting their role as that of co-rulers.

Exclusive worship of YHWH as recognition of his unique identity

Alongside these two principal ways of characterizing God's unique identity we must set an indication of the unique identity of God which plays a different, but essential, role in Jewish monotheism. This is monolatry, the exclusive worship of the one God. There is no doubt that in religious practice this was the factor which most clearly signalled the distinction between God and all other reality.[16] God must be worshipped; no other being may be worshipped.[17] The pervasive concern of Jews in

[14] Isa. 57:15; 3 Macc. 2:2; *4 Ezra* 8:20–21; *2 Enoch* 20:3J.

[15] E.g. *1 Enoch* 14:18–22.

[16] R. Bauckham, 'Jesus, Worship of', *ABD* 3. 816 ('Judaism was unique among the religions of the Roman world in demanding the exclusive worship of its God. It is not too much to say that Jewish monotheism was defined by its adherence to the first and second commandments'); idem, *The Climax of Prophecy: Studies on the Book of Revelation* (Edinburgh: T. & T. Clark, 1993) 118; idem, *The Theology of the Book of Revelation* (Cambridge: Cambridge University Press, 1993) 58–59.

[17] For the slender evidence adduced for some kind of veneration of angels by Jews see L. Stuckenbruck, *Angel Veneration and Christology*

the Second Temple period for the uniqueness of their God can be seen in their scruples about any practice which could be construed as worship of humans or other beings regarded as gods by others.[18] From all non-Jews who believed in or worshipped a high god but never supposed this to be incompatible with the worship also of lesser divinities, Jews were sharply distinguished by their monolatrous practice.[19]

Some recent argument has tended to the position that the exclusive worship of the one God is really the factor that defines God as unique in Second Temple Judaism.[20] This, in my view, is a confusion, because the exclusive worship of the God of Israel is precisely *a recognition of and response to* his unique identity. It is God's unique identity which requires worship of him alone. Worship of other beings is inappropriate because they do not share in this unique identity. Worshipping God, along with withholding worship from any other being, is recognition of the absolute distinction between God and all other reality.

The distinction in cultic practice between Jews and others who acknowledged a high god is in fact correlative with a

---

17 *(continued)* (WUNT 2/70; Tübingen: Mohr [Siebeck], 1995) 45–203; C. E. Arnold, *The Colossian Syncretism* (Grand Rapids: Baker Books, 1996) 32–89. While there may be a few marginal instances of the worship of angels, as there is plentiful evidence of the invocation of angels in magical practice, it is very doubtful whether any substantial number of Jews treated angels in a way that they would themselves have regarded as comparable, even in degree, with the worship of God. Occasional prayer to angels should not be confused with worship.

18 Add. Est. 13:12–14; Philo, *Leg. Gai.* 116; cf. Acts 10:25–26.

19 See J. M. G. Barclay, *Jews in the Mediterranean Diaspora from Alexander to Trajan (323 BCE – 117 CE)* (Edinburgh: T. & T. Clark, 1996) 429–434.

20 Hurtado, 'What Do We Mean', 348–368. This takes his attempt to give worship the key role in the definition of Jewish monotheism further than his earlier *One God*. I tended to this view myself in R. Bauckham, 'Jesus, Worship of ', *ABD* 3. 816: 'Judaism was unique among the religions of the Roman world in demanding the exclusive worship of its God. It is not too much to say that Jewish monotheism was defined by its adherence to the first and second commandments.'

difference in monotheistic conception. The typical Hellenistic view was that worship is a matter of degree because divinity is a matter of degree. Lesser divinities are worthy of appropriate degrees of worship. Philosophical monotheists, who held that all other divine being derives ultimately from the One, nevertheless held the derived divinity of lesser divine beings to be appropriately acknowledged in cultic worship. The notion of a hierarchy or spectrum of divinity stretching from the one God down through the gods of the heavenly bodies, the daemons of the atmosphere and the earth, to those humans who were regarded as divine or deified, was pervasive in all non-Jewish religion and religious thought, and inseparable from the plurality of cultic practices in honour of a wide variety of divinities. Jews understood their practice of monolatry to be justified, indeed required, because the unique identity of YHWH was so understood as to place him, not merely at the summit of a hierarchy of divinity, but in an absolutely unique category, beyond comparison with anything else. Worship was the recognition of this unique incomparability of the one God. It was the response to YHWH's self-revelation as the sole Creator and Ruler of all.

Hence in Second Temple Judaism monolatry was not a substitute for the lack of a clear concept of divine uniqueness. It was the corollary of a notion of God's unique identity which itself was carefully framed so as to indicate the absolute distinction between God and all other reality. The requirement of exclusive worship and the common ways of characterizing the unique identity of God correlated with and reinforced each other. On the one hand, that it is inappropriate to worship beings other than the one God could be justified by pointing out that all such beings are created by him, benefit humans only in a way that derives ultimately from God, and are ministers of God's will, not independent sources of good.[21] In other words, they do not participate in the unique identity of God the Creator and Ruler of all things and therefore do not deserve worship, which is acknowledgement of that unique identity.

---

[21] E.g. Josephus, *Ant.* 1.155–156; *2 Enoch* 66:4–5[J]; *Sib. Or.* 3:20–35.

On the other hand, when some Hellenistic philosophical accounts of the one supreme God as the sole source of all other being and providential overseer of all things correspond quite closely to Jewish monotheistic ideas,[22] the language of such accounts can be borrowed by some Jewish writers. In this case, the formal definition of the unique identity of the one God may be closely similar, but the Jewish claim that such a God requires exclusive worship heightens the significance of the distinction being made between the one God and all other reality. Whereas the tendency of non-Jewish thought is to assimilate such ideas of divine uniqueness to patterns of thought in which the supreme God is the summit of a hierarchy of divinity, or the original source of a spectrum of divinity, the tendency of Jewish thought is to accentuate the absolute distinction between God and all else as the dominant feature of the whole Jewish world-view. The deeply rooted Jewish sense that the unique identity of God required exclusive worship played an important role in this difference.

Jewish monotheism and 'intermediary' figures

The evidence that Jews of this period could easily and were in the habit of drawing a firm line of clear distinction between the one God and all other reality is far more considerable than the small amount of evidence adduced by those who argue that so-called intermediary figures blur this distinction. Methodologically, it is imperative to proceed from the clear consensus of Second Temple monotheism to the more ambiguous evidence about so-called intermediary figures to which we now turn. The question that needs to addressed in the case of such figures is: By the criteria which Second Temple Jewish texts themselves constantly use to distinguish the one God from all other reality, do these figures belong to the unique identity of God or do they fall outside it? Are they, so to speak, intrinsic to God's own unique identity as the one God, or are they creatures and

[22] See, for example, the doctrine of God in the Pseudo-Aristotelian treatise *De Mundo*, summarized by R. M. Grant, *Gods and the One God* (London: SPCK, 1986) 78–79.

servants of God, however exalted? The criteria which count are the criteria by which Jews of the period themselves distinguished the unique identity of God, not other possible criteria of divinity which were not the decisive ones for them. Once these criteria are applied, it seems to me that in almost every case the question I have just asked is readily answerable. In other words, some of these figures are unambiguously depicted as intrinsic to the unique identity of God, while others are unambiguously excluded from it. Unfortunately, there is no space here to argue the case in the way that it requires to be argued, by examining the texts in detail. All that is possible in the present context is to outline the argument very broadly.

Two categories of intermediary figures can be distinguished. The first has been called principal angels and exalted patriarchs.[23] These are angelic or human figures who play a very important role in God's rule over the world. They are either very high-ranking angels, such as Michael in the Qumran literature or Yahoel in the *Apocalypse of Abraham*, or human figures such as Moses in the work of Ezekiel the Tragedian or the Son of Man in the *Parables of Enoch*, if it is correct to think that that work identifies the Son of Man with Enoch exalted to heaven. The second category of intermediary figures consists of personifications or hypostatizations of aspects of God himself, such as his Spirit, his Word and his Wisdom. (Because of their relevance to early Christology, I shall confine the present discussion to Word and Wisdom.) In my view, the Jewish literature in question for the most part unequivocally excludes the figures in the first category from the unique identity of God, while equally unequivocally including the figures in the second category within the unique identity of God.

'Intermediary' figures: principal angels and exalted patriarchs

Applying our criteria, there is no suggestion anywhere in the literature that principal angels or exalted patriarchs participate

---

[23] Hurtado, *One God*, 17.

in the work of creation. They are clearly created beings.[24] With regard to God's sovereignty over the cosmos, Second Temple Jewish literature does certainly envisage a small group of very highly placed angels,[25] who form a kind of council of chief ministers of state, each in charge of some major aspect of the divine government of the cosmos.[26] This picture has been distorted by the assertion in much recent scholarship that the literature frequently envisages a single principal angel (though the identity of this angel varies in various texts), a sort of grand vizier or plenipotentiary, to whom God delegates the whole of his rule over the cosmos.[27] In my view such a figure appears in very few[28] of the texts. A less than careful reading of the texts has mistakenly manufactured such a figure. For example, in some works the archangel Michael, who is the heavenly patron of Israel, takes precedence as first in rank among the principal angels.[29] This corresponds to the pre-eminent position of Israel in God's rule over the world. But it does not mean that Michael is in charge of all the work of all the other angels. There is no

---

24 For angels as created, see *Jub.* 2:2; *Bib. Ant.* 60:2; *2 Bar.* 21:6; *2 Enoch* 29:3; 33:7.

25 Seven in *1 Enoch* 20:1–8; Tob. 12:15; Rev. 8:2; four in *1 Enoch* 9:1; 10:1–11; 40:3–10; 54:6; 71:8–9; 1QM 9:15–16; *Ap. Mos.* 40:3.

26 E.g. *1 Enoch* 20:2–8; 40:9.

27 E.g. A. F. Segal, *Two Powers in Heaven* (SJLA 25; Leiden: Brill, 1977) 186–200; Hurtado, *One God*, 71–82; P. Hayman, 'Monotheism: A Misused Word in Jewish Studies?', *JJS* 42 (1991) 11; Barker, *The Great Angel*.

28 I find the idea of a single vicegerent of God in only the following cases, where special considerations can be seen to be at work: the archangel (probably Michael) in *Joseph and Aseneth*, where his role in heaven is modelled on Joseph's in Egypt (14:8–9; cf. Gen. 45:8); the Spirit of truth or Prince of light (also identified with Michael) in some Qumran texts (especially 1QS 3:15–4:1), where the role is due to the rather distinctive features of Qumran dualism; and the Logos in Philo, who had his own philosophical-theological reasons for envisaging a single mediator of all divine relationship to the world. The other so-called intermediary figures have much more limited roles.

29 *1 Enoch* 40:9; cf. *T. Mos.* 10:1; 1QM 17:7–8.

suggestion, for example, that the angels who are in charge of the workings of nature, an extremely important part of the angelic activity in the world, come under the supervisory authority of Michael. Michael ranks higher than the other principal angels, but he is not set in authority over their spheres of government. So the notion of a heavenly viceroy, who is next to God in charge of the cosmos, as a standard idea in the Jewish conception of the cosmos is a fiction. This alleged precedent for Christology should be forgotten.

The most exalted angels serve God; they do not participate in his rule. Two features, among others, make this clear. In the first place, they never sit with God on his heavenly throne, the obvious symbol which Jewish writers could have used, in their depictions of the heavens, to portray a viceroy or co-ruler. On the contrary, they stand, in the posture of servants.[30] Secondly, not only are they never worshipped, but they explicitly reject worship. They are portrayed as doing so in a series of texts which form a stereotyped literary tradition, clearly designed to distinguish exalted angels, who declare themselves mere servants of God, from God.[31] These texts clearly deploy the criteria of sovereignty and worship to draw the line between God who rules all things and should therefore be worshipped, and, on the other hand, glorious heavenly beings who, being only servants of God, may not be worshipped.

There is one exception which proves the rule. In the Parables of Enoch, the Son of Man will in the future, at the eschatological day of judgement, be placed by God on God's own throne

---

[30] Tob. 12:15; *T. Abr.* A7:11; 8:1–4; 9:7–8; cf. also Luke 1:19.

[31] The clearest examples in Jewish literature are Tob. 12:16–22; *Apoc. Zeph.* 6:11–15; *3 Enoch* 16:1–5; *Cairo Genizah Hekhalot* A/2, 13–18, and in Christian literature Rev. 19:10; 22:8–9; *Ascen. Isa.* 7:18–23; 8:1–10; *Ap. Paul* [Coptic ending]; *Apocryphal Gos. Matt.* 3:3; cf. also *2 Enoch* 1:4–8; *3 Enoch* 1:7; *Lad. Jac.* 3:3–5; Jos. *Asen.* 14:9–12; 15:11–12. They are studied in R. Bauckham, 'The Worship of Jesus in Apocalyptic Christianity', *NTS* 27 (1980–81) 322–341; revised version in idem, *The Climax*, chapter 4; see also L. T. Stuckenbruck, 'An Angelic Refusal of Worship: The Tradition and Its Function in the Apocalypse of John', *SBLSP* 1994, 679–696; idem, *Angel Veneration*, 75–103.

to exercise judgement on God's behalf.[32] He will also be worshipped.[33] This is the sole example of an angelic figure or exalted patriarch who has been included in the divine identity: he participates in the unique divine sovereignty and therefore, in recognition of his exercise of the divine sovereignty, he receives worship. His inclusion in the divine identity is partial, since he plays no part in the work of creation or indeed in the divine sovereignty until the future day of judgement, and therefore his inclusion in the divine identity remains equivocal. But he is the only such equivocal case, which shows, by contrast, the absence in other cases of any of the criteria by which Second Temple Jews would consider a heavenly figure to share the divine identity.[34]

'Intermediary' figures: personified or hypostatized divine aspects

The second category of intermediary figures – personifications or hypostatizations of aspects of God – turns out by the same

---

[32] *1 Enoch* 61:8; 62:2, 5; 69:27, 29; cf. 51:3.

[33] 46:5; 48:5; 62:6, 9. This worship cannot be understood as merely an expression of submission to a political superior, since the Son of Man is seated on the throne of God. In such a context it is recognition of the unique divine sovereignty over the world.

[34] A second case is frequently alleged: Moses in the *Exagoge* of Ezekiel the Tragedian (68–89), but in my view this passage has been widely misunderstood. Moses in a dream sees himself replacing God on the throne of the universe. Raguel's interpretation of the dream takes this to be a symbol of Moses' career as a king and prophet of Israel. What God is in relation to the cosmos, Moses will be in relation to Israel. Ezekiel is offering an interpretation of the statement in Exod 7:1 that Moses' God will make Moses 'God'. The dream depicts this literally (God vacates his own cosmic throne and places Moses on it), but the meaning of the dream is its interpretation as a metaphor of Moses' earthly role. Cf. Gen. 37:9–10: in Joseph's dream he receives the worship the heavenly bodies give to God, but the meaning of the dream is that his parents and brothers will serve him.

criteria to be quite different. Both the Word and the Wisdom of God take part in the work of creation, sometimes with distinguishable roles,[35] sometimes interchangeably.[36] The texts in question make it quite clear that they are not infringing the standard monotheistic insistence that God created without assistance of any kind.[37] *2 Enoch* 33:4, in an echo of Deutero-Isaiah (Isa. 40:13),[38] says that God had no advisor in his work of creation, but that his Wisdom was his advisor. The meaning is clearly that God had *no one* else to advise him. His Wisdom, who is not someone else but intrinsic to his own identity, advised him. Similarly, Wisdom is depicted sitting on the great divine throne beside God, participating in the exercise of his sovereignty by playing the role of advisor or counsellor to the king (*1 Enoch* 84:2–3; Wis. 9:4, 10). Here the image which the literature refrains from applying to any angelic servant of God is applied to Wisdom, with no detriment to the clear distinction between God and all other reality, because precisely this symbol serves to include Wisdom in the unique identity of the one God who rules the cosmos from his uniquely exalted throne. In general, the personifications of God's Word and God's Wisdom in the literature are not parallel to the depictions of exalted angels as God's servants. The personifications have been developed precisely out of the ideas of God's own Wisdom and God's own Word, that is, aspects of God's own identity. In a variety of ways they *express* God, his mind and his will, in relation to the world. They are not created beings, but nor are they semi-divine entities occupying some ambiguous status between the one God and the rest of reality. They belong to the unique divine identity.

My conclusion that the Word and the Wisdom of God are intrinsic to the unique divine identity, as understood in Jewish

---

35 Ps. 33:9; 4 *Ezra* 6:38; *2 Bar.* 56:3–4; *2 Enoch* 33:4.

36 **Wisdom**: Jer. 10:12; 51:15; Ps. 104:24; Prov. 3:19; 8:30; Sir. 24:3b, Wis. 7:22; 8:4–6; cf. 1QH 9:7, 14, 20; Wis. 9:2; **Word**: Ps. 33:6; Sir. 42:15; *Jub.* 12:4; *Sib. Or.* 3:20; *2 Bar.* 14:17; 21:4; 48:8; *4 Ezra* 6:38; *T. Abr.* A9:6; Wis. 9:1.

37 Isa. 44:24; *2 Enoch* 33:4; *4 Ezra* 3:4; Josephus, *C. Ap.* 2.192.

38 Cf. Sir. 42:21; *1 Enoch* 14:22; Wis. 9:13, 17; 1QS 11:18–19.

monotheism, does not decide the question (which, in my view, must be secondary) whether the personification of these figures in the literature is merely a literary device or whether they are envisaged as having some form of distinct existence in reality. I think there is a good argument for the latter at least in some of the texts about Wisdom (e.g. Wis. 7:22–8:1). But this does not mean that Wisdom is there envisaged as a subordinate divine being extrinsic to the identity of the one God. It means that these Jewish writers envisage some form of real distinction within the unique identity of the one God. If so, they are not abandoning or in any way compromising their Jewish monotheism. The Second Temple Jewish understanding of the divine uniqueness does not define it as unitariness and does not make distinctions within the divine identity inconceivable. Its perfectly clear distinction between God and all other reality is made in other terms, which in this case place God's Wisdom unequivocally within the unique divine identity.

Chapter Two

Christological Monotheism in the New Testament

Chapter Two

Christological Monotheism in the New Testament

Divine identity Christology

In the previous chapter I outlined an analysis of the nature of Second Temple Jewish monotheism, arguing that the unique identity of the God of Israel is the category by means of which we can best grasp the way Jews of the period understood God. I argued that the Judaism of the period was pervasively, self-consciously, and strictly monotheistic, in the sense of having a clear concept of the absolute distinction between God and all other reality, with extensive implications for religious practice. The uniqueness of the divine identity was characterized especially by two features: that the one God is sole Creator of all things and that the one God is sole Ruler of all things. To this unique identity corresponds monolatry, the exclusive worship of the one and only God who is so characterized. Worship, in the Jewish tradition, is recognition of the unique divine identity, and so must be accorded to the one who created and rules all things, but may not be accorded to any other beings, all of whom are created by and subject to the one true God. Finally, I argued (without being able to present the evidence in detail) that the so-called intermediary figures which feature in some Jewish texts of the period do not, as is often alleged, blur or bridge the line of absolute distinction which Jewish monotheism maintained between God and all other reality. On the contrary, if we allow the texts to operate, as they do, Judaism's own criteria of distinction between God and all other reality, we find that, almost without exception, these figures belong unambiguously either outside the unique identity of God, so that there is no proper Jewish sense in which they count as divine, or else within the unique identity of God, such that they are intrinsic to God's own identity as the one God. Principal angels and exalted patriarchs do not participate in the unique creative work of God, nor do they participate in the exercise of God's rule by sharing the divine throne; they merely carry out God's will as servants, and so they are not worshipped. The Word and the Wisdom of God, on the other hand, do participate in the creative work of God and in his sovereignty, and so belong intrinsically to God's unique identity. In neither case, once we understand the way Jewish monotheism drew the distinction between God and all other reality, is there any blurring of the line.

The present chapter will build on this understanding of Jewish monotheism an argument about New Testament Christology. Once again, there is no possibility of providing more than a small sampling of the evidence for this case, which ought properly to encompass all the important christological texts of the New Testament. I shall concentrate on illustrating a way of reading the texts which puts the whole question of the character of New Testament Christology in a new light. In this argument the understanding of Jewish monotheism which I have proposed will function as the hermeneutical key to understanding the way in which the New Testament texts relate Jesus Christ to the one God of Jewish monotheism. It will enable us to see that the intention of New Testament Christology, throughout the texts, is to include Jesus in the unique divine identity as Jewish monotheism understood it. The writers do this deliberately and comprehensively by using precisely those characteristics of the divine identity on which Jewish monotheism focused in characterizing God as unique. They include Jesus in the unique divine sovereignty over all things, they include him in the unique divine creation of all things, they identify him by the divine name which names the unique divine identity, and they portray him as accorded the worship which, for Jewish monotheists, is recognition of the unique divine identity. In this way they develop a kind of christological monotheism which is fully continuous with early Jewish monotheism but distinctive in the way it sees Jesus Christ himself as intrinsic to the identity of the unique God.

I shall be arguing what will seem to anyone familiar with the study of New Testament Christology a surprising thesis: that the highest possible Christology, the inclusion of Jesus in the unique divine identity, was central to the faith of the early church even before any of the New Testament writings were written, since it occurs in all of them. Although there was development in understanding this inclusion of Jesus in the identity of God, the decisive step of so including him was made at the beginning of Christology. Essential to this argument is the recognition that this high Christology was entirely possible within the understanding of Jewish monotheism we have outlined. Novel as it was, it did not require any repudiation of the monotheistic faith which the first Christians axiomatically shared with all Jews. That Jewish monotheism and high Christology were in some way in tension is one of the prevalent illusions in this field that we must allow the texts to dispel. The New Testament writers did not see their Jewish monotheistic heritage as in any way an obstacle to the inclusion of Jesus in the divine identity; they used its resources extensively in order precisely to include Jesus in the divine identity; and they saw in this inclusion of Jesus in the divine identity the fulfilment of the eschatological expectation of Jewish monotheism that the one God will be universally acknowledged as such in his universal rule over all things.

As I observed at the beginning of chapter 1, recent attempts to make high Christology intelligible as a development within a thoroughly Jewish context have focused on the so-called intermediary figures as providing precedents or parallels for high Christology. The conviction has been that a direct identification of Jesus with the one God would have been impossible for Jewish monotheism, whereas the various figures alleged to occupy ambiguous or semi-divine status, participating in divinity in some subordinate way, make room within Jewish monotheism for the attribution of divine attributes and functions to Jesus. This conviction is in my view almost the exact opposite of the truth. What Jewish monotheism could not accommodate were precisely semi-divine figures, subordinate deities, divinity by delegation or participation. The key to the way in which Jewish monotheism and high Christology were compatible in the early Christian movement is not the claim that Jewish monotheism left room for ambiguous semi-divinities, but the recognition that its understanding of the unique identity of the one God left room for the inclusion of Jesus in that identity. Though such a step was unprecedented, the character of Jewish monotheism did not make it impossible. Moreover, it was not a step which could be, as it were, approached gradually by means of ascending christological beliefs. To put Jesus in the position, for example, of a very high-ranking angelic servant of God would not be to come close to a further step of assimilating him to God, because the absolute distinction between God and all other reality would still have to be crossed. The decisive step of including Jesus in the unique identity of God was not a step that could be facilitated by prior, less radical steps. It was a step which, whenever it were taken, had to be taken simply for its own sake and *de novo*. It does not become any more intelligible by being placed at the end of a long process of christological development. In my view, the New Testament evidence is best explained if this step was taken very early as the fundamental step on which all further christological development then rested.

The exalted Jesus participates in God's unique sovereignty over all things

At a very early stage, which is presupposed and reflected in all the New Testament writings, early Christians understood Jesus to have been exalted after his death to the throne of God in the highest heaven. There, seated with God on God's throne, Jesus exercises or participates in God's unique sovereignty over the whole cosmos. This decisive step of understanding a human being to be participating now in the unique divine sovereignty over the cosmos was unprecedented. The principal angels and exalted patriarchs of Second Temple

Jewish literature provide no precedent. It is this radical novelty which leads to all the other exalted christological claims of the New Testament texts. But, although a novelty, its meaning depends upon the Jewish monotheistic conceptual context in which the early Christians believed it. Because the unique sovereignty of God over all things was precisely one of the two major features which characterized the unique identity of God in distinction from all other reality, this confession of Jesus reigning on the divine throne was precisely a recognition of his inclusion in the unique divine identity, himself decisively distinguished, as God himself is, from any exalted heavenly servant of God. We shall see further evidence of this as we proceed.

Psalm 110:1 in early Christology

Early Christian theology, like other Jewish theology of the period, proceeded primarily by exegesis of the Hebrew scriptures. Creative exegesis of the scriptures was the principal medium in which early Christians developed even the most novel aspects of their thought, a point of which we shall have to take much notice in later parts of this book. But the point is important now, because the participation of Jesus in the unique divine sovereignty was understood primarily by reference to one key Old Testament text (Ps. 110:1) and other texts brought into exegetical relationship with it. Psalm 110:1 (LXX 109:1) is the Old Testament text to which the New Testament most often alludes (twenty-one quotations or allusions, scattered across most of the New Testament writings,[1] with the Johannine literature the one notable exception). It reads

---

[1] Matt. 22:44; 26:64; Mark 12:36; 14:62; 16:19; Luke 20:42–43; 22:69; Acts 2:33–35; 5:31; 7:55–56; Rom. 8:34; 1 Cor. 15:25; Eph. 1:20; 2:6; Col. 3:1; Heb. 1:3, 13; 8:1; 10:12–13; 12:2; 1 Pet. 3:22; Rev. 3:21. All these allusions are certain, except Rev. 3:21, which is probable.

The LORD said to my Lord,
'Sit at my right hand
until I make your enemies your footstool'.[2]

The verse certainly does not have to be read as meaning that the person referred to as 'my Lord' (the Messiah) is seated on the divine throne itself and exercises the divine sovereignty over the cosmos. It could, for example, be read to mean simply that the Messiah is given a position of honour as a favoured subject beside the divine throne, where he sits inactively awaiting the inauguration of his rule on earth. This is how some of the rabbis later read it.[3] It is quite clear, however, that early Christians read it differently: as placing Jesus on the divine throne itself, exercising God's own rule over all things. The point is sometimes made by combining the verse with Psalm 8:6:

You made him ruler over the works of your hands
and placed all things under his feet.[4]

The discontinuity between early Christology at this decisive point and the beliefs and expectations of Second Temple Jewish literature can be illustrated from the fact that, whereas Psalm 110:1 is the most quoted Old Testament text in the New Testament, in the whole of the literature of Second Temple Judaism there is only one probable allusion to the verse, in the *Testament of Job* (33:3),[5] where its use bears little resemblance

[2] On the early Christian use of this text, see D. H. Hay, *Glory at the Right Hand: Psalm 110 in Early Christianity* (SBLMS 18; Nashville: Abingdon, 1973); M. Hengel, 'Sit at My Right Hand!', in idem, *Studies in Early Christology* (Edinburgh: T. & T. Clark, 1995) 119–225.

[3] Hay, *Glory*, 28–31.

[4] Ps. 110:1 and Ps. 8:6 conflated or associated: Matt. 22:44; Mark 12:36; 1 Cor. 15:25–28; Eph. 1:20–22; 1 Pet. 3:22; cf. Heb. 1:13–2:9.

[5] The point is that, in place of his throne and splendour in this world, which is passing away, Job has an eternal splendour reserved for him in heaven. The point is not to give him a position of authority in

to its significance for early Christians. Nowhere in early Judaism is it applied to one of the exalted heavenly figures – angels or patriarchs – who occupy important places in heaven now or in the future. Nowhere is it applied to the Messiah, who is never, of course, supposed in early Jewish expectation to rule the cosmos from heaven, but only to be a ruler on earth. The messianic interpretation of the royal psalms in general would lead us to expect that, when Jews in the Second Temple period did interpret Psalm 110, they would apply it to the Messiah. But its absence from the literature shows that it had no importance for them, whereas for early Christians it was of key importance. The difference simply reflects the fact that early Christians used the text to say something about Jesus which Second Temple Jewish literature is not interested in saying about anyone: that he participates in the unique divine sovereignty over all things.

My argument is that the exaltation of Jesus to the heavenly throne of God could only mean, for the early Christians who were Jewish monotheists, his inclusion in the unique identity of God, and that furthermore the texts show their full awareness of that and quite deliberately use the rhetoric and conceptuality of Jewish monotheism to make this inclusion unequivocal. As evidence for this I will refer to four further aspects of the way the texts envisage the exaltation of Jesus.

Jesus' sovereignty over 'all things'

First, the texts frequently refer to Jesus' exaltation or sovereignty as over 'all things'. Though New Testament scholars commonly fail to recognize this and in individual texts debate the extent of the 'all things' to which the text refers, the

---

[5] *(continued)* God's rule over the world, but to depict his heavenly reward as the eternal reality of which his kingdom in this world has been only a worthless shadow. This provides no precedent for early Christian use of the text, in which Christ's enthronement at God's right hand is not merely his individual heavenly reward but his unique cosmic status and role.

phrase belongs to the standard rhetoric of Jewish monotheism, in which it constantly refers, quite naturally, to the whole of the created reality from which God is absolutely distinguished as its Creator and Ruler.[6] God's servants may be said, by his permission, to rule some things, as earthly rulers do, but only God rules over all things from a throne exalted above all things. The frequent New Testament christological uses of this phrase[7] should not be studied atomistically, but their cumulative weight should be appreciated as testimony to the way the texts habitually define Christ's exaltation or rule in the terms Jewish monotheism reserved for God's unique sovereignty.

Jesus shares God's exaltation above all the angelic powers

Secondly, many of the texts emphasize Jesus' exaltation and sovereignty over all the angelic powers, sometimes with emphatic use of the potent Jewish imagery of height. For example, Ephesians 1:21–22:

> [God] raised [Jesus] from the dead and seated him at his right hand in the heavenly places, far above all rule and authority and power and dominion, and above every name that is named, not only in this age but also in the age to come. And he has put all things under his feet . . .

---

[6] E.g. Isa. 44:24; Jer. 10:16; 51:19; Sir. 43:33; Wis. 9:6; 12:13; Add. Est. 13:9; 2 Macc. 1:24; 3 Macc. 2:3; *1 Enoch* 9:5; 84:3; *2 Enoch* 66:4; *Jub.* 12:19; *Apoc. Abr.* 7:10; *Jos. Asen.* 12:1; *Sib. Or* 3:20; 8:376; Frag 1:17; Josephus, *BJ* 5.218; 1QapGen 20:13; 4QD[b] 18:5:9.

[7] For Christ's lordship over 'all things', see Matt. 11:27; Luke 10:22; John 3:35; 13:3; 16:15; Acts 10:36; 1 Cor. 15:27–28; Eph. 1:22; Phil. 3:21; Heb. 1:2; 2:8; cf. Eph. 1:10, 23; 4:10; Col. 1:20. For Christ's participation in the creation and sustaining of 'all things', see John 1:3; 1 Cor. 8:6; Col. 1:16–17; Heb. 1:3.

That 'far above' evokes the image of the high and lofty divine throne at the summit of the heavens (cf. also Eph. 4:10), exalted far above the various angelic powers which rule as God's servants in the lower heavens.[8] Jesus is not here being placed in the position of any angelic figure, nor are the angelic powers being demoted. The spatial relationship between Jesus on the divine throne and the angelic powers is precisely how Jewish pictures of the heavenly realms portrayed the relationship between the divine throne and the angelic powers subject to God. The point is that Jesus now shares God's own exaltation and sovereignty over every angelic power. Similarly in the great christological passage in Hebrews 1, where a catena of seven scriptural quotations is deployed to explicate the full meaning of Psalm 110:1, with which the catena concludes, the significance of Jesus' exaltation to the right hand of God is expounded by proving his superiority over all the angels. This superiority is both imaged as spatial height (1:3–4) and expounded as qualitative difference. The angels, argues the passage, are no more than servants of God, whereas Christ, who occupies the divine throne itself, participates in God's own sovereignty and is therefore served by the angels (1:7–9, 13–14). The purpose is not a polemic against angels or angel Christology. Nothing that is said about the angels would have been controversial to any Jewish reader. The function of the angels in the passage is to assist theological definition of the one God, to portray the line of distinction which Jewish monotheism always insisted on drawing between God the only sovereign Ruler and all other reality. When this line is drawn, even the highest angels are only servants of God. Of course. But if Jesus is superior to the angels, participating in the divine sovereignty, this means, precisely for Jewish monotheistic conceptuality, that he is included in the unique identity of the one God. Careful study of Hebrews 1, for which we lack space here, would reveal with what care and sophistication the passage employs all the key features by which Jewish

---

[8] Cf. especially *T. Levi* 3:4: 'In the highest of all [the heavens] dwells the Great Glory in the holy of holies far above every holiness.'

monotheism standardly characterized the uniqueness of God in order to include Jesus within the unique divine identity.

Jesus given the divine name

Thirdly, the exalted Jesus is given the divine name, the Tetragrammaton (YHWH), the name which names the unique identity of the one God, the name which is exclusive to the one God in a way that the sometimes ambiguous word 'god' is not. Hebrews 1:4 states that Jesus, exalted to the right hand of God, became 'as much superior to the angels as the name he has inherited is more excellent than theirs'. Though most of the commentators do not think so, this can only refer to the divine name, as must 'the name that is above every name', which according to Philippians 2:9 was bestowed on Jesus when God exalted him to the highest position. Connected with this naming of the exalted Jesus by the divine name is the early Christian use of the phrase 'to call on the name of the Lord',[9] as a reference to Christian confession and to baptism. The Old Testament phrase[10] means to invoke God by his name YHWH,[11] but the early Christian use of it applies it to Jesus. It means invoking Jesus as the divine Lord who exercises the divine sovereignty and bears the divine name.

Worship of Jesus as recognition of his exercise of the unique divine sovereignty

Fourthly, the exalted Christ's participation in the unique divine sovereignty is recognized by worship. As we observed in chapter 1, worship in the Jewish tradition is recognition of the unique divine identity. It is accorded to God especially as

[9] Acts 2:17–21, 38; 9:14; 22:16; Rom. 10:9–13; 1 Cor. 1:2; 2 Tim. 2:22.
[10] Note especially Ps. 80:18; Isa. 12:4; Joel 2:32; Zeph. 3:9; Zech. 13:9.
[11] Cf. Gen. 4:26; 1 Kgs. 18:24–39.

sole Creator of all things and as sole Ruler of all things. It most obviously puts into religious practice the distinction Jewish monotheism drew between the one God and all other reality. So the significant christological evidence is not only that which shows, as has been increasingly recognized in recent scholarship, that the practice of worshipping Jesus goes far back into early Jewish Christianity, but also the evidence that worship was thought to be due to Christ precisely as response to his inclusion in the unique divine identity through exaltation to the throne of God. Therefore very significant are the depictions of universal worship in Philippians 2:9–11 and Revelation 5, two passages we shall consider in more detail in the next chapter. In both it is precisely the exaltation of Christ to the divine throne which evokes the worship of all creation. Also noteworthy is Matthew 28:17, where, in the closing scene of this Gospel, the disciples worship Jesus as he declares that all authority in heaven and on earth has been given to him.[12]

The pre-existent Christ participates in God's unique activity of creation

The evidence we have considered so far amounts to what could be called christological and eschatological monotheism. Jesus is seen as the one who exercises God's eschatological sovereignty over all things, with a view to the coming of God's kingdom and the universal acknowledgement of God's unique deity. Jesus is included, we might say, in the *eschatological* identity of God. Clearly the dominant early Christian concern was with Jesus' present and future participation in the divine sovereignty. It is therefore all the more remarkable that early Christians included Jesus in the unique divine sovereignty not only eschatologically but also protologically, not only in the present and future, but also from the beginning. This must be mainly because for Jewish monotheism the eternal divine sovereignty, including God's unique creative activity in the beginning as well as his providential ordering of all things and

[12] Note also Heb. 1:6; John 5:21–23.

his future completion of his purpose for his reign over all things, is properly indivisible. God alone rules all things and will rule all things because he alone created all things. If Jesus is no mere servant of God but participates in the unique divine sovereignty and is therefore intrinsic to the unique divine identity, he must be so eternally. The participation of Christ in the creative work of God is necessary, in Jewish monotheistic terms, to complete the otherwise incomplete inclusion of him in the divine identity. It also makes it even clearer that the intention of this early Christology is to include him in the unique divine identity, since in the creative work of God there was for Jewish monotheists no room even for servants of God to carry out his work at his command. Creation, axiomatically, was the sole work of God alone.

Whereas the inclusion of Jesus in the eschatological sovereignty of God is found in all the New Testament literature, his inclusion in the work of creation is less widespread, but is found in 1 Corinthians, Colossians, Hebrews, Revelation and the Gospel of John.[13] Since it is of less direct relevance to most of the concerns of the New Testament writers, this is not surprising. What is noteworthy is that in three of these cases (1 Corinthians, Hebrews, and John) the purpose, in my view, is precisely to express Jewish monotheism in christological terms. It is not that these writers wish to say anything about the work of creation for its own sake or even that they wish to say anything about the relationship of Christ to creation for its own sake, but that they wish to include Jesus Christ in the unique divine identity. Including him precisely in the divine activity of creation is the most unequivocal way of excluding any threat to monotheism – as though Jesus were a subordinate demi-god – while redefining the unique identity of God in a way that includes Jesus. To illustrate the point, we shall examine the earliest of these texts: 1 Corinthians 8:6. This passage in its context reads:

---

[13] John 1:1–5; 1 Cor. 8:6; Col. 1:15–16; Heb. 1:2–3, 10–12; Rev. 3:14.

> [4]Hence, as to the eating of food offered to idols, we know that 'there is no idol in the world' and that 'there is no God except one'. [5]Indeed, even though there may be so-called gods in heaven or on earth – as in fact there are many gods and many lords – [6]but for us there is one God, the Father, from whom are all things and we for him, and one Lord, Jesus Christ, through whom are all things and we through him.

Paul's concern in this context is explicitly monotheistic. The issue of eating meat offered to idols and participation in temple banquets is an instance of the highly traditional Jewish monotheistic concern for loyalty to the only true God in a context of pagan polytheistic worship. What Paul does is to maintain this Jewish monotheistic concern in a Christian interpretation for which loyalty to the only true God entails loyalty to the Lord Jesus Christ. He takes up from the Corinthians' letter (at the end of verse 4) the typical Jewish monotheistic formula 'there is no God except one' in order to agree with it and to give, in verse 6, his own fuller monotheistic formulation, which contrasts the 'many gods and many lords' of the Corinthians' pagan environment (verse 5) with the one God and one Lord to whom Christians owe exclusive allegiance.

Verse 6 is a carefully formulated statement:

a but for us [there is] one God, the Father,
b from whom [are] all things and we for him,
c and one Lord, Jesus Christ,
d through whom [are] all things and we through him.

The statement has been composed from two sources, both clearly recognizable. One is the *Shema'*, the classic Jewish statement of the uniqueness of God, taken from the Torah itself, recited twice daily by all observant Jews, as we noticed in chapter 1. It is now commonly recognized that Paul has here adapted the *Shema'* and produced, as it were, a Christian version of it.[14] Not so widely recognized is the full significance

---

[14] F. F. Bruce, *1 and 2 Corinthians* (NCB; London: Oliphants, 1971) 80; D. R. de Lacey, ' "One Lord" in Pauline Christology', in H. H.

of this. In the first and third lines of Paul's formula (labelled a and c above), Paul has in fact reproduced all the words of the statement about YHWH in the *Shema'* (Deut. 6:4: 'The LORD our God, the LORD, is one'),[15] but Paul has rearranged the words in such a way as to produce an affirmation of both one God, the Father, and one Lord, Jesus Christ. It should be quite clear that Paul is including the Lord Jesus Christ in the unique divine identity. He is redefining monotheism as christological monotheism. If he were understood as *adding* the one Lord to the one God of whom the *Shema'* speaks, then, from the perspective of Jewish monotheism, he would certainly be producing not christological monotheism but outright ditheism. The *addition* of a unique Lord to the unique God of the *Shema'* would flatly *contradict* the uniqueness of the latter. The only possible way to understand Paul as maintaining monotheism is to understand him to be including Jesus in the unique identity of the one God affirmed in the *Shema'*. But this is in any case clear from the fact that the term 'Lord', applied here to Jesus as the 'one Lord', is taken from the *Shema'* itself. Paul is not adding to the one God of the *Shema'* a 'Lord' the *Shema'* does not mention. He is identifying Jesus as the 'Lord' whom the *Shema'* affirms to be one. Thus, in Paul's quite unprecedented reformulation of the *Shema'*, the unique identity of the one God *consists of* the one God, the Father, *and* the one Lord, his Messiah. Contrary to what many exegetes who have not sufficiently understood the way in which the unique identity of God was understood in Second Temple Judaism seem to suppose, by including Jesus in this unique

---

14 *(continued)* Rowdon ed., *Christ the Lord* (D. Guthrie FS; Leicester: Inter-Varsity Press, 1982) 191–203; Dunn, *Christology*, 180; Hurtado, *One God*, 97; N. T. Wright, *The Climax of the Covenant* (Edinburgh: T. & T. Clark, 1991) 128–129; D. A. Hagner, 'Paul's Christology and Jewish Monotheism', in M. Shuster and R. Muller ed., *Perspectives on Christology* (P. K. Jewett FS; Grand Rapids: Zondervan, 1991) 28–29; N. Richardson, *Paul's Language about God* (JSNTSup 99; Sheffield: JSOT Press, 1994) 300; B. Witherington, *Jesus the Sage* (Edinburgh: T. & T. Clark, 1994) 316.

15 The 'our' of the *Shema'* appears as the 'for us' at the beginning of Paul's reformulation.

identity Paul is certainly *not* repudiating Jewish monotheism, whereas were he merely associating Jesus with the unique God, he certainly *would* be repudiating monotheism.

Whereas the first and third lines of the formulation divide the wording of the *Shema'* between God and Jesus, the second and fourth lines (labelled b and d above) similarly divide between God and Jesus another Jewish monotheistic formula, one which relates the one God as Creator to all things. The description in its undivided, unmodified form is used elsewhere by Paul, specifically in Romans 11: 36a: 'from him and through him and to him [are] all things'. Here the statement simply refers to God, whereas in 1 Corinthians 8:6 Paul has divided it between God and Christ, applying to God two of the prepositions that describe God's relationship as Creator to all things ('from' and 'for' or 'to') and the third of these prepositions ('through') to Christ. Although Paul's formula in Romans 11:36 does not appear precisely in this form elsewhere, there are enough Jewish parallels[16] to make it certain that Paul there simply quotes a Jewish formulation. That God is not only the agent or efficient cause of creation ('from him are all things') and the final cause or goal of all things ('to him are all things'), but also the instrumental cause ('through him are all things') well expresses the typical Jewish monotheistic concern that God used no one else to carry out his work of creation, but accomplished it alone, solely by means of his own Word and/or his own Wisdom. Paul's reformulation in 1 Corinthians 8:6 includes Christ in this exclusively divine work of creation by giving to him the role of instrumental cause.

Implicit in the reformulation is an identification of Christ with either the Word or the Wisdom of God or both. It hardly matters which, since the Jewish habit of explaining God's sole creative work by saying that he created through his word or through his wisdom merely gives Paul the opportunity for apportioning the work of creation in such a way as to include Christ in it. We can now see that in this and other New Testament passages where the pre-existent Christ is described

---

[16] Josephus, *BJ* 5.218; Philo, *Cher.* 127; cf. Heb. 2:10.

in terms corresponding to Jewish language about the Word or the Wisdom of God, it is not the Jewish concepts of Word and Wisdom themselves which are driving the christological development. The purpose is to include Jesus completely in the unique identity of God, protologically as well as eschatologically. The role of the Word and/or Wisdom was appropriate for this purpose, since, as we saw in chapter 1, they represent Jewish ways of making some form of distinction within the unique divine identity, especially with reference to the work of creation. Their activity in creation by no means compromises the monotheistic uniqueness of the divine creative activity since they are intrinsic to the unique divine identity. This is exactly what Paul means to say of Jesus. In the passage in 1 Corinthians, Paul exhibits the typically strong Jewish monotheistic self-consciousness; he distinguishes the one God to whom alone allegiance is due from all pagan gods who are no gods; he draws on classic Jewish ways of formulating monotheistic faith; and he reformulates them to express a christological monotheism which by no means abandons but maintains precisely the ways Judaism distinguished God from all other reality and uses these to include Jesus in the unique divine identity. He maintains monotheism, not by adding Jesus to but by including Jesus in his Jewish understanding of the divine uniqueness.

Conclusion: New Testament Christology as Christology of Divine Identity – beyond 'functional' and 'ontic' Christology

A higher Christology than Paul already expresses in 1 Corinthians 8:6 is scarcely possible, and the way I have just summed it up may stand as a summary of what a much more extensive review of the christological material throughout the New Testament would show to be the common character of all New Testament Christology. In conclusion to this chapter, I shall point out the general significance of the category of divine identity as I have used it as the key to understanding New Testament Christology, by contrast with the categories which have dominated discussion of New Testament Christology in recent decades, which are so-called 'functional' Christology and so-called 'ontic' (or ontological) Christology. A Christology of divine identity will take us, I suggest, beyond the fundamentally misleading contrast between 'functional' and 'ontic' Christology as categories for reading the New Testament texts. In my view, these categories have proved inadequate to the task of illuminating the texts, not least because they do not reflect an adequate understanding of the way Jewish monotheism understood God.

Thus, for example, while much of what we have observed in this chapter about the New Testament's portrayal of Jesus' participation in the unique sovereignty of God has been observed before, its full significance has been largely missed through reliance on misleading presuppositions and use of inappropriate categories. The dominance of the distinction between 'functional' and 'ontic' Christology has made it seem unproblematic to say that for early Christology Jesus exercises the 'functions' of divine lordship without being regarded as 'ontically' divine. In fact, such a distinction is highly problematic from the point of view of early Jewish monotheism, for in this understanding of the unique divine identity, the unique sovereignty of God was not a mere 'function' which God could delegate to someone else. It was one of the key identifying characteristics of the unique divine identity, which distinguished the one God from all other reality. The unique divine sovereignty is a matter of *who God is*. Jesus' participation in the unique divine sovereignty is therefore also not just a matter of what Jesus does, but of *who Jesus is* in relation to God. Though not primarily a matter of divine nature or being, it emphatically *is* a matter of divine identity. It includes Jesus in the identity of the one God. When extended to include Jesus in the creative activity of God, and therefore also in the eternal transcendence of God, it becomes unequivocally a matter of regarding Jesus as *intrinsic* to the unique identity of God.

The distinction commonly made between 'functional' and 'ontic' Christology has been broadly between early Christology in a Jewish context and patristic Christology which applied Greek philosophical categories of divine nature to

Christ. Even when ontic Christology is seen to begin well within the confines of the New Testament, it is seen as the beginnings of the patristic attribution of divine nature to Christ. The assumption usually is that whereas first-century Jewish monotheists could attribute divine 'functions' to Jesus without difficulty, since this would not infringe Jewish monotheism, they could not easily attribute divine 'nature' to him without raising difficult issues for monotheism with which only later trinitarian developments could cope (successfully or not). However, this is to misconstrue Jewish monotheism in Hellenistic terms as though it were primarily concerned with *what divinity is* – divine nature – rather than with *who YHWH, the unique God, is* – divine identity. The whole category of divine identity and Jesus' inclusion in it has been fundamentally obscured by the alternative of 'functional' and 'ontic', understood to mean that either Christology speaks simply of what Jesus does or else it speaks of his divine nature. Once the category of divine identity replaces those of function and nature as the primary and comprehensive category for understanding both Jewish monotheism and early Christology, then we can see that the New Testament's lack of concern with the divine nature of Christ is by no means an indication of a merely functional Christology. We can see that throughout the New Testament texts there is a clear and deliberate use of the characteristics of the unique divine identity to include Jesus in that identity. Once we have rid ourselves of the prejudice that high Christology must speak of Christ's divine nature, we can see the obvious fact that the Christology of divine identity common to the whole New Testament is the highest Christology of all. It identifies Jesus as intrinsic to who God is.

Chapter Three

God Crucified: The Divine Identity Revealed in Jesus

Chapter Three

God Crucified: The Divine Identity Revealed in Jesus

From the exalted and pre-existent Christ to the earthly Jesus

In the first two chapters I have argued that, if we attend carefully and accurately, on the one hand, to the ways in which Second Temple Judaism characterized the unique identity of the one and only God, and, on the other hand, to what New Testament writers say about Jesus, it becomes abundantly clear that New Testament writers include Jesus in the unique identity of the one God. They do so carefully, deliberately, consistently and comprehensively by including Jesus in precisely those divine characteristics which for Second Temple Judaism distinguished the one God as unique. All New Testament Christology is in this sense very high Christology, stated in the highest terms available in first-century Jewish theology. It is certainly not a merely functional Christology, but is, I have suggested, best characterized as a Christology of divine identity. Jesus, the New Testament writers are saying, belongs inherently to *who God is*.

My argument so far has been designedly selective in two ways. In the first place, I have focused on those features of the identity of the God of Israel which Second Temple Judaism regularly highlighted as characterizing the uniqueness of God by distinguishing God absolutely from all other reality: notably, that God is the Creator of all things and sovereign Ruler of all things. Other features of the identity of the God of Israel, which I pointed out in the first chapter were essential to Jewish understanding of God, were nevertheless left aside in my argument so far because they were not the aspects to which Jews were accustomed to appeal in defining the uniqueness of the one God. Secondly, in illustrating the way in which New Testament writers employ these key features of the unique identity of God in order to include Jesus in it, I have focused on the pre-existent Christ, who participated in the creative activity of God, and on the exalted Christ, who at the right hand of God participates in God's eschatological sovereignty over all things. To the earthly Jesus, his life and death, I have not referred, because it is the pre-existent and exalted Christ who most obviously shares in the unique creative and sovereign relationship of God to all other reality. It was in Jesus' exaltation to share the divine throne in heaven that the early Christians recognized his inclusion in the divine identity.

However, we now reach the stage of my argument in which it is appropriate to consider the earthly Jesus, and this will also in due course bring into play those other essential features of the identity of the God of Israel which have not so far figured in my christological argument. Initially, however, focusing on the earthly Jesus turns the issue of the divine identity around. For the early Christians, the inclusion of the exalted Jesus in the divine identity meant that the Jesus who lived a truly and fully human life from conception to death, the man who suffered rejection and shameful death, also belonged to the unique divine identity. What did this say about the divine identity? Whereas hitherto we have considered what the New Testament writers' understanding of the relation of Jesus to God says about Jesus, we must now ask what it says about God. In other words, we must consider Jesus as the revelation of God. The profoundest points of New Testament Christology occur when the inclusion of the exalted Christ in the divine identity entails the inclusion of the crucified Christ in the divine identity, and when the christological pattern of humiliation and exaltation is recognized as revelatory of God, indeed as the definitive revelation of who God is. Such a revelation could not leave the early Christian understanding of God unaffected, but at the same time the God whose identity the New Testament writers understood to be now defined by the history of Jesus was undoubtedly the God of Israel. His identity in Jesus must be consistent with his identity in the Hebrew scriptures. So, with the New Testament writers, we shall have to identify the continuity within the novelty, the already known identity of the God of Israel in the newly revelatory history of Jesus.

Christological monotheism: The early Christian reading of Isaiah 40–55

Within the limited space available, I shall pursue just one approach to the way New Testament writers understood the inclusion of the earthly life and death of Jesus within the identity of God. As we have noticed in chapter 2, much of the creative theological thinking in earliest Christianity was done by way of Old Testament exegesis. The writers did theologically creative exegesis in the Jewish tradition. They did not, of course, read the Jewish scriptures in the historicizing manner of modern Old Testament scholarship, but nor did they, as some accounts of New Testament interpretation of the Old seem to suggest, simply read into the Old Testament ideas they held in any case independently of the Old Testament. They brought the Old Testament text into relationship with the history of Jesus in a process of mutual interpretation from which some of their profoundest theological insights sprang.

No part of the Old Testament was more important to them than the chapters we know as Deutero-Isaiah (Isaiah 40–55). (Of course, for early Christians these chapters were simply part of the book of the prophet Isaiah, but the term Deutero-Isaiah can serve as a convenient label for this section of the book, which they would certainly have seen as a distinguishable section of Isaiah's prophecy.) For the early Christians, these chapters of Isaiah, above all, were the God-given account of the significance of the events of eschatological salvation which they had witnessed and in which they were involved: Isaiah's vision of the new Exodus, the divine act of redemption of Israel in the sight of all the nations and also for the sake of the nations themselves, leading to, in the chapters we call Trito-Isaiah, the new Jerusalem and the new creation of all things. The New Testament writers' extensive indebtedness to Deutero-Isaiah has been widely acknowledged, even if its precise extent has been debated. The fact that the very word 'Gospel' was taken by the earliest Christians from Deutero-Isaiah (Isa. 40:9) is an indication of the key importance of these chapters for them, as is the fact that all four evangelists highlight the way the beginning of the Gospel story, the ministry of John the Baptist, fulfilled the beginning of Deutero-Isaiah's prophecy of the new Exodus (Isa. 40:3–4).[1] What has not been recognized sufficiently is that, behind many of the New Testament texts, lies an integrated early Christian reading of these chapters as a connected whole. Allusions to the narrative of the Suffering Servant in chapter 53, for example, should not be read as though early Christian use of this one chapter is sufficient to explain them, nor only in connexion with the other Servant passages in Deutero-Isaiah, but as integral to a reading of Isaiah 40–55 as a prophecy of the new Exodus which leads to the salvation of the nations.

For our purposes it is important to notice the way in which the monotheistic theme in Deutero-Isaiah coheres with the themes of these chapters as a whole. Outside the great monotheistic texts of the Torah, the divine speeches in Deutero-Isaiah constitute the classic monotheistic sources of Second Temple Judaism. The speeches in which God declares his uniqueness ('I am the LORD and there is no other'), asserting it polemically against the idols who are no gods, defining his uniqueness as Creator of all things and sovereign Ruler of history, contain all the characteristics of divine uniqueness which we considered in chapter 1. It was in the unique identity of this God of Deutero-Isaiah, in his cosmic and historical lordship, that early Christians so clearly and deliberately included the pre-existent and exalted Christ. But the monotheism of Deutero-Isaiah is also eschatological. It looks to the day when the God of Israel will demonstrate himself to be the one and only God in the sight of all the nations, revealing his glory

[1] Matt. 3:3; Mark 1:2–3; Luke 3:4–6; John 1:23.

and his salvation in the deliverance of his people, so that all the ends of the earth will acknowledge him as God and turn to him for salvation. It is in his great act of eschatological salvation, the new Exodus, that the one and only God will demonstrate his unique deity universally. This is also the coming of his kingdom, announced by the messenger who brings good news (the Gospel) of salvation, saying to Zion, 'Your God reigns' (Isa. 52:7; cf. 40:9). The one God implements his universal sovereignty in the new Exodus which demonstrates his deity to the nations. It was in this context of the necessary link between the uniqueness of God and his eschatological acts for the salvation of Israel and the world that the early Christians read of the enigmatic figure of the Servant of the Lord, who witnesses to God's unique deity and who, in chapters 52–53, both suffers humiliation and death and also is exalted and lifted up.

What I hope to show is that in the early Christian reading of Deutero-Isaiah, the witness, the humiliation, the death and the exaltation of the Servant of the Lord are the way in which God reveals his glory and demonstrates his deity to the world. The witness, the humiliation and the exaltation of the Servant are the eschatological salvation event, the new Exodus, by which the unique deity of God is now identified, such that the ends of the earth acknowledge that God is God and turn to him for salvation when they see the exaltation of his Servant. One important key to this early Christian reading of Deutero-Isaiah, in my view, lies in the connexions between Isaiah 52:13, which introduces the crucial passage about the Suffering Servant, and other passages of Isaiah. The three relevant texts in translations of both their Hebrew original and their Greek version are:

Isaiah 52:13 Hebrew: Behold, my Servant shall prosper; he shall be *exalted (yārûm)* and *lifted up (niššā')* and shall be very high *(gāvah)*.

LXX Greek: Behold, my Servant shall understand, and shall be *exalted (hupsōthēsetai)* and shall be *glorified (doxasthēsetai)* greatly.

Isaiah 6:1 Hebrew: . . . I saw the Lord *(ᵃdōnai)* sitting on a throne, *exalted (rām)* and *lofty (niśśā')*; and his train filled the temple.
LXX Greek: . . . I saw the Lord sitting on a throne, *exalted (hupsēlou)* and lifted up *(epērmenou)*; and the house was full of his glory.

Isaiah 57:15 Hebrew: For thus says the *exalted (rām)* and *lofty (niśśā')* One who inhabits eternity, whose name is Holy: 'I dwell in the *high (mārôm)* and holy place, and also with those who are crushed (*dakkā'* cf. Isa. 53:5, 10) and lowly in spirit, to revive the spirit of the lowly and to revive the heart of the crushed.'
LXX Greek: Thus says the Most High *(hupsistos)* who dwells in the heights *(en hupsēlois)* for ever, Holy among the holy ones *(en hagiois)* is his name, the Most High *(hupsistos)* resting among the holy ones *(en hagiois)*, and giving patience to the faint-hearted, and giving life to the broken-hearted.

Isaiah 52:13 states, with emphasis, the exaltation of the Servant, presumably following the humiliation and death described in the following passage. There are two points to notice about it: (1) The words 'exalted' and 'lifted up' ('my Servant shall be exalted and lifted up') occur also in Isaiah 6:1, introducing Isaiah's vision of God on his throne (where the throne is described as 'exalted and lifted up'), and in Isaiah 57:15, which describes God, dwelling in the heights of heaven, as himself 'exalted and lifted up'. The combination of the two Hebrew roots *rûm* (to be high, to be exalted) and *nāśā'* (to lift up) is rare in the Hebrew Bible, and the verbal coincidence between these three verses is striking. Modern Old Testament scholars think the two later passages, Isaiah 52:13 and 57:15, must be dependent on Isaiah 6:1. Early Christians would have observed the coincidence and applied the Jewish exegetical principle of *gezērâ šāvâ*, according to which passages in which the same words occur should be interpreted with reference to each other. (In my view, most early Christian exegesis of the Old Testament was done with reference to the Hebrew text, even when the Greek text was also employed. In this case, the texts can be connected on the basis of the Septuagint Greek translation, but are more strikingly connected in the Hebrew.)

So, in the light of the connexions with Isaiah 6:1 and 57:15, the meaning of Isaiah 52:13 is that the Servant is exalted to the heavenly throne of God. This is why, in John 12:38–41, Isaiah 53 and Isaiah 6 are brought together, and Isaiah is said to have seen Jesus' glory, meaning that he did so when he saw the glory of the Lord in his vision in chapter 6 of his prophecy. (2) If Isaiah 52:13 means that the Servant was exalted to share the heavenly throne from which God rules the universe, then it is readily connected with Psalm 110:1, which was, as we have seen in chapter 2, the central Old Testament text for the early Christian inclusion of Jesus in the identity of God. Therefore two New Testament references to the exaltation of Jesus to the right hand of God combine allusion to Psalm 110:1 with allusion to Isaiah 52:13 (Acts 2:33; 5:31) and one combines allusion to Psalm 110:1 with allusion to Isaiah 57:15 (Heb. 1:3).

The Servant, in both his humiliation and his exaltation, is therefore not merely a human figure distinguished from God, but, in both his humiliation and his exaltation, belongs to the identity of the unique God. This God is not only the high and lofty one who reigns from his throne in the high and holy place; he also abases himself to the condition of the crushed and the lowly (Isa. 57:15). And when the nations acknowledge his unique deity and turn to him for salvation, it is the Servant, humiliated and now exalted to sovereignty on the divine throne, whom they acknowledge.

Christological monotheism in three examples of the Christian reading of Isaiah 40–55: (1) Philippians 2:6–11

We now turn to three parts of the New Testament in which we can see this reading of Deutero-Isaiah reflected and developed in particular ways: Philippians 2:6–11, the book of Revelation, and the Gospel of John.

First we shall see how in each of these three parts of the New Testament monotheistic motifs from Deutero-Isaiah are applied to Jesus. These are some of the most remarkable instances of the inclusion of Jesus in the unique identity of the one God who declares his uniqueness in the divine speeches of Deutero-Isaiah. Each has been noticed before, but separately. What has gone unnoticed is the convergence of Paul, Revelation and the Fourth Gospel in this inclusion of Jesus in Deutero-Isaianic monotheism.

Philippians 2:6–11 is one of the central christological passages of the Pauline literature, and therefore also one of the earliest passages of christological reflection that we have in the New Testament. The climax of the passage is reached when Jesus is exalted to the position of divine sovereignty over all things and given the divine name itself, which names the unique divine identity,

> so that at the name of Jesus
> *every knee should bend,*
> In heaven and on earth and under the earth,
> [11]*and every tongue should acknowledge*
> that Jesus Christ is Lord,
> to the glory of God the Father (vv. 10–11).

The allusion (indicated by the italics above) is to Isaiah 45:22–23:

> Turn to me and be saved,
> all the ends of the earth!
> For I am God, and there is no other.
> By myself I have sworn,
> from my mouth has gone forth in righteousness
> a word that shall not return:
> 'To me every knee shall bow,
> every tongue shall swear'.

We should note the characteristic Old Testament and especially Deutero-Isaianic assertion of the absolute uniqueness of YHWH: 'I am God and there is no other.' This passage in Deutero-Isaiah depicts – indeed it is *the* passage in Deutero-Isaiah which depicts – the eschatological demonstration of YHWH's unique deity to the whole world. This is the point at which the one Creator of all things and Sovereign over all things proves himself to be so, acknowledged as both only God and only Saviour by all the ends of the earth which turn to him in worship and for salvation. The Philippians passage is therefore no unconsidered echo of an Old Testament text, but a claim that it is in the exaltation of Jesus, his identification as YHWH in YHWH's universal sovereignty, that the unique deity of the God of Israel comes to be acknowledged as such by all creation. Precisely Deutero-Isaianic *monotheism* is fulfilled in the revelation of Jesus' participation in the divine identity. Eschatological monotheism proves to be christological monotheism.[2]

Christological monotheism in three examples of the Christian reading of Isaiah 40–55: (2) Revelation

Secondly, we turn to a set of titles which the book of Revelation applies both to God and to Jesus Christ:[3]

[God says] I am the Alpha and the Omega (1:8).
[Christ says] I am the first and the last (1:17; cf. 2:8).
[God says] I am the Alpha and the Omega,
the beginning and the end (21:6).
[Christ says] I am the Alpha and the Omega,
the first and the last,
the beginning and the end (22:13).

The three phrases – the Alpha and the Omega, the first and the last, the beginning and the end – are clearly treated as equivalent phrases (since alpha and omega are the first and last letters of the Greek alphabet), and are claimed both by

[2] I have argued this view of Philippians 2:9–11 more fully in R. Bauckham, 'The Worship of Jesus in Philippians 2:9–11', in R. P. Martin and B. J. Dodd ed., *Where Christology Began: Essays on Philippians 2* (Louisville: Westminster/John Knox, 1998) 128–139.
[3] For a more detailed treatment, see R. Bauckham, *The Theology of the Book of Revelation* (Cambridge: Cambridge University Press, 1993) 25–28, 54–58.

God (1:8; 21:6) and by Christ (1:17; 22:13), in declarations of unique divine identity strategically located in the opening and closing sections of the book. These declarations are modelled on those of YHWH in Deutero-Isaiah (44:6; 48:12; cf. 41:4):

> Isa. 44:6 I am the first and I am the last; besides me there is no God.
>
> Isa. 48:12 I am he; I am the first, and I am the last.

The four declarations in Revelation form a deliberately cumulative pattern, in which the first three declarations attribute different, though equivalent, phrases to God and Christ respectively, but in which the fourth declaration claims for Christ all three forms of the title. One form of the title ('the first and the last') is attributed only to Christ, but the other two ('the Alpha and the Omega, the beginning and the end') are attributed to both God and Christ. Indeed, they are the only title shared by both God and Christ in the book of Revelation. They say something significant about this work's inclusion of Jesus in the unique divine identity.

In the form, 'the first and the last', the title comes from Deutero-Isaiah, where it is one of the terms that encapsulates Deutero-Isaianic monotheism. It expresses the unique eternal sovereignty of the one God, who precedes all things as their Creator and as the Lord of history brings all things to their eschatological fulfilment. He is the source and the goal of all things. Revelation thus includes Christ both protologically and eschatologically in the identity of the one God of Deutero-Isaianic monotheism. Indeed, it is to Christ rather than to God that it attributes the specifically Deutero-Isaianic form of the title, 'the first and the last', on which the other two forms are variations. Once again, Deutero-Isaianic monotheism is interpreted as christological monotheism. God proves to be not only the first but also the last, the end, the Omega of all things, when his kingdom comes in that coming of Christ towards which the whole book of Revelation is orientated.

Christological monotheism in three examples of the Christian reading of Isaiah 40–55: (3) Gospel of John

It is the eschatological orientation of the book of Revelation, directed to the future achievement of the unique sovereignty of the one God, which makes the title 'the first and the last' particularly appropriate, among the monotheistic motifs of Deutero-Isaiah, for christological use in that book. The Gospel of John understandably makes a different choice when it places on the lips of Jesus during his ministry another of the characteristically Deutero-Isaianic declarations of unique divine identity. The Johannine choice is the concise statement 'I am he,' in Hebrew *'ănî hû'*, usually translated in the Septuagint Greek as *egō eimi* ('I am'), the form in which it appears in John's Gospel.[4] This sentence occurs as a divine declaration of unique identity seven times in the Hebrew Bible: once in Deuteronomy, in one of the most important monotheistic passages of the Torah, and six times in Deutero-Isaiah.[5] It serves to declare, in the most concise of forms, the uniqueness of God, equivalent to the more common 'I am YHWH'. On the lips of Jesus in the Fourth Gospel, its ambiguity, in contexts where it need not be recognized as the uniquely divine self-declaration, enables it to identify Jesus with God, not in a blatantly explicit way which, even in the Fourth Gospel, would be inappropriate before Jesus' exaltation, but in a way which becomes increasingly unambiguous through the series of seven absolute 'I am' sayings (John 4:26; 6:20; 8:24, 28, 58; 13:19; 18:5, 6, 8). It is certainly not accidental that, whereas in the Hebrew Bible there are seven occurrences of *'ănî hû'* and two of the emphatic variation *'ānokî 'ānokî hû'* (Isa. 43:25; 51:12), in John there are seven absolute 'I am' sayings, with the seventh repeated twice (18:5, 6, 8) for the sake of an emphatic climax (thus seven or nine in both cases). The series of sayings thus comprehensively identifies Jesus with the God of Israel who sums up his identity in the declaration 'I

---

[4] P. B. Harner, *The 'I Am' of the Fourth Gospel* (Facet Books; Philadelphia: Fortress, 1970); D. M. Ball, *'I Am' in John's Gospel* (JSNTSup 124; Sheffield: Sheffield Academic Press, 1996).

[5] Deut. 32:39; Isa. 41:4; 43:10, 13; 46:4; 48:12; 52:6.

am he'. More than that, these sayings identify Jesus as the eschatological revelation of the unique identity of God, predicted by Deutero-Isaiah.

So in these three major representatives of New Testament Christology – Philippians 2:6–11, Revelation, John – we see, in different forms, the early Christian interpretation of Deutero-Isaiah's eschatological monotheism as christological monotheism. The use of monotheistic motifs from Deutero-Isaiah in these passages of high christological reflection shows that monotheism is not an incidental concern, but a central concern in the Christology of these texts. Moreover, the application of monotheistic motifs from Deutero-Isaiah to Jesus means more than his inclusion in the unique identity of God. It means that he is the revelation of that unique identity of God to the world. So far from the inclusion of Jesus in divinity constituting a problem for monotheism, these New Testament writers present it as the way in which the unique God demonstrates his unique divinity to the world.

The humiliation and exaltation of Jesus revealing the divine identity in three examples of the Christian reading of Isaiah 40–55: (1) Philippians 2:5–11

What we must now investigate, as the second stage of our argument in relation to all three of these New Testament texts, is the way they present the suffering, humiliation and death of Jesus in Deutero-Isaianic terms closely related to the monotheistic motifs from Deutero-Isaiah. Jesus fulfils the eschatological monotheism of the prophecies because he is the Servant of the Lord of Deutero-Isaiah whose humiliation and exaltation together reveal the identity of the one God.

Philippians 2:6–11 is the subject of one of the most complex exegetical debates in New Testament scholarship.[6] I cannot

[6] An invaluable survey of scholarship is in R. P. Martin, *Carmen Christi: Philippians 2:5–11 in Recent Interpretation and in the Setting of Early Christian Worship* (revised edition; Grand Rapids: Eerdmans, 1983); and, most recently, in R. P. Martin and B. J. Dodd ed., *Where Christology Began*.

here argue all the disputed issues, but will merely indicate the positions I take on some of the key exegetical points as preliminary to the theme I want to draw out for our present purposes. (1) Against the majority view that the passage is a pre-Pauline hymn, I am inclined to think Paul himself composed it. So I shall speak of the author as Paul, but the issue makes no difference to my exegesis. (2) Against those recent interpreters who think that from the outset the passage concerns the human Jesus, I maintain the traditional view, still that of the majority of exegetes and vindicated in most recent discussions,[7] that the passage begins by speaking of the pre-existent Christ in eternity and proceeds to speak of his incarnation. (3) I do not think the passage embodies an Adam Christology. If Adam is in view at all, he is in view only very indirectly. In my view Adam has proved a red herring in study of this passage. (4) On the difficult translation issue of the meaning of verse 6b, I think the best linguistic argument now suggests the translation: 'he did not think equality with God something to be used for his own advantage'. In other words, the issue is not whether Christ gains equality or whether he retains it, as in some translations. He has equality with God and there is no question of losing it; the issue is his attitude to it.[8] (5) The 'form of God' (v 6) and the 'form of a servant (slave)' (v 7), which clearly are intended to be contrasted, refer to forms of appearance: the splendour of the divine glory in heaven contrasted with the human form on earth.[9]

These preliminary exegetical decisions result in the following exegesis of verses 6–11. The pre-existent Christ, being equal with God, shared the divine glory in heaven. But he did

---

[7] D. Hurst, 'Re-Enter the Pre-Existent Christ in Philippians 2:5–11?', *NTS* 32 (1986) 449–457; C. A. Wanamaker, 'Philippians 2.6–11: Son of God or Adam Christology', *NTS* 33 (1987) 179–193; Wright, *The Climax of the Covenant* (Edinburgh: T. & T. Clark, 1991) 56–98 (but in my view Wright is trying to have his cake and eat it in combining a divine incarnational and an Adam christological approach).

[8] Wright, *The Climax*, 62–90.

[9] Wanamaker, 'Philippians 2.6–11', 183–187.

not consider his equality with God something he should use for his own advantage. He did not understand his equality with God as a matter of being served by others, but as something he could express in service, obedience, self-renunciation and self-humiliation for others. Therefore he renounced the outward splendour of the heavenly court for the life of a human being on earth, one who lived his obedience to God in self-humiliation even to the point of the peculiarly shameful death by crucifixion, the death of a slave. This radical self-renunciation was his way of expressing and enacting his equality with God, and *therefore* (v 9) it qualified him to exercise the unique divine sovereignty over all things. His exaltation to the highest position, the heavenly throne of God, is not a matter of gaining or regaining equality with God, which he has always had and never lost, but of acquiring the function of implementing the eschatological sovereignty of God. Exercising the unique divine sovereignty, he bears the unique divine name, the Tetragrammaton, and receives the worship of the whole creation. Since he had expressed his equality with God in a human life of obedient service to God, his exercise of the divine sovereignty also does not compete with his Father's deity, but redounds to the glory of his Father (v 11). This is the way in which the one and only God reveals his identity to his whole creation and is acknowledged as God by his whole creation.

To fill out this basic exegesis, I will make three further points: (1) What is going on in this passage is a profound interpretation of Deutero-Isaiah. The allusion to Isaiah 45 in verses 10–11 we have already discussed: it is universally agreed, though its full significance is by no means always appreciated. More debatable is the allusion to Isaiah 52–53 in verses 7–9, but I think the verbal connexions are easily strong enough to establish such allusion.[10] The most important are as follows:

---

[10] Cf. L. Cerfaux, 'Hymne au Christ – Serviteur de Dieu (*Phil.*, II, 6–11 = *Is.*, LII, 13-LIII, 12)', in *Receuil Lucien Cerfaux: Études d'Exégèse et d'Histoire Religieuse*, vol. 2 (BETL 6–7; Gembloux: Duculot, 1954) 425–437.

Philippians 2:6–11	Isaiah 52–53; 45
[Christ Jesus], though he was in the form of God, did not regard equality with God as something to be used for his own advantage,	
[7]but *poured himself out*, taking the *form* of a slave, being born in human *likeness*; and being found in human *form*, [8]he *humiliated* himself, becoming obedient *to the point of accepting death* – even death on a cross.	53:12: because he poured himself out . . . (52:14; 53:2: form . . . appearance) (53:7: he was brought low) 53:12: . . . to death.
[9]*Therefore* also God *exalted him to the highest place* and conferred on him the Name that is above every name, [10]so that at the name of Jesus *every knee should bend*, in heaven and on earth and under the earth, [11]*and every tongue should acknowledge* that Jesus Christ is Lord, to the glory of God the Father.	53:12: Therefore . . . 52:13: he shall be exalted and lifted up and shall be very high. 45:22–23: Turn to me and be saved, all the ends of the earth! For I am God, and there is no other. [23]By myself I have sworn, from my mouth has gone forth in righteousness a word that shall not return 'To me every knee shall bow, every tongue shall swear'.

What has not been noticed, even by those who see that Paul has the Suffering Servant of Isaiah 53 in view here, is the way the allusions to Isaiah 52–53 and to Isaiah 45 cohere. Paul is reading Deutero-Isaiah to mean that the career of the Servant of the Lord, his suffering, humiliation, death and exaltation, is the way in which the sovereignty of the one true God comes to be acknowledged by all the nations.

The key verse in Isaiah 53 is verse 12, the concluding verse of the passage: '*Therefore* I will allot him a portion with the great . . . *because* he poured out himself to death . . .' The prophet says that *because* the Servant humiliated himself, *therefore* God exalted him. This is precisely the message and the structure of the Philippians passage. Verses 7–8 of the passage are Paul's exegesis of the second of those two clauses in Isaiah 53:12 ('because he poured out himself to death'). Paul understands this clause to summarize the whole movement of the Servant's self-renunciation and self-humiliation, ending in death, and so he expands it by inserting further explanation between 'he poured himself out' (which in Paul's Greek is a literal translation of Isaiah's Hebrew[11]) and 'to death'. The pouring out or emptying is the self-renunciation in service and obedience, which begins with incarnation and leads inexorably to death. Paul then glosses the word 'death' (from Isaiah) with the phrase 'even death on a cross' to indicate that the form of death was this appropriately shameful end to the self-humiliation already described in Isaiah 53. But Isaiah says that because the Servant poured himself out, therefore God will exalt him ('allot him a portion with the great'), a theme already announced at the beginning of the Isaianic passage (52:12): 'my servant shall be exalted and lifted up, and shall be very high'. Paul echoes this verse in his verse 9 ('Therefore God exalted him to the highest place'), and, understanding it in the way we have already explored, to mean that the Servant was exalted to the divine throne, he adds that he receives the divine name. The Servant thus exalted to the divine throne is the one to whom the ends of the earth turn in acknowledgement of his unique divine identity, according to Isaiah 45.

(2) The central themes of the passage are the relation between high and low status, and between service and lordship. Certainly, one who belongs to the unique divine identity ('equal with God') becomes also human, but the issue is not seen in terms of a contrast between divine and human natures. The question is not: how can the infinite God become a finite creature, how can the omnipotent, omniscient and omnipresent God take on human limitations, how can the immortal God die? These questions arise when the contrast of divine and

[11] J. Jeremias, 'Zu Phil. 2,7: ΕΑΥΤΟΝ ΕΚΕΝΩΣΕΝ', *NovT* 6 (1963) 182–188.

human natures comes to the fore, as it did in the patristic period. Here in Philippians 2 the question is rather one of status. Can the one who inhabits the heights of heaven, high on his throne above all creation, come down not merely to the human level, but even to the ultimate degradation: death on a cross? Can he renounce the form of God, the honour and glory of divine status in the heavenly palace, where the myriads of angels serve him, for the form of a servant, the dishonour, the loss of all status, that a human life that ends on a cross entails? The self-humiliation and obedience to which verse 8 refers are no mere ethical attitudes, but the repudiation of status, the acceptance of the slave's lack of status, the voluntary descent to the place furthest removed from the heavenly throne to which he is then – and Paul says 'therefore' – exalted. This is not the contrast of two natures, divine and human, but a contrast more powerful for first-century Jewish theology with its controlling image of God as the universal emperor, high on his heavenly throne, inconceivably exalted above all he has created and rules. Can the cross of Jesus Christ actually be included in the identity of this God?

Can the Lord also be the Servant? The passage, inspired both by Deutero-Isaiah and by the Christ-event, answers: only the Servant can also be the Lord.

(3) The passage amounts to a christological statement of the identity of God. The exaltation of Christ to participation in the unique divine sovereignty shows him to be included in the unique divine identity. But since the exalted Christ is first the humiliated Christ, since indeed it is *because* of his self-abnegation that he is exalted, his humiliation belongs to the identity of God as truly as his exaltation does. The identity of God – who God is – is revealed as much in self-abasement and service as it is in exaltation and rule. The God who is high can also be low, because God is God not in seeking his own advantage but in self-giving. His self-giving in abasement and service ensures that his sovereignty over all things is also a form of his self-giving. Only the Servant can also be the Lord. Only the Servant who is also the Lord receives the recognition of his lordship – the acknowledgement of his unique deity – from the whole creation.

The humiliation and exaltation of Jesus revealing the divine identity in three examples of the Christian reading of Isaiah 40–55: (2) Revelation

We turn now more briefly to the second of our three New Testament examples of reading Isaiah 40–55 in relation to the humiliation and exaltation of Jesus: the book of Revelation. Chapter 4 of the book depicts, like many another apocalyptic disclosure, the great divine throne in heaven on which the One who created all things sits. The rest of the book reveals his purpose for achieving his eschatological sovereignty over the creation in which his rule is presently contested. Chapter 5, the continuation of the vision of the divine throne in heaven, reveals in a preliminary way how this will occur and anticipates its result: the worship of God by every creature in the whole creation. The scene is a close parallel to Philippians 2. John sees the exalted Christ on the divine throne, represented in his vision as a lamb standing as though it were slaughtered. The lamb receives the worship of the heavenly attendants just as God had in chapter 4, but now the circle of worship expands, so that every creature in heaven and on earth and under the earth and in the sea worships 'the One who is seated on the throne and the lamb' (verse 13). Thus it is the enthronement of the slaughtered lamb, his exercise of the divine sovereignty, which leads to the universal acknowledgement of the God to whose identity he belongs. The lamb is undoubtedly the Passover lamb and belongs to the image of eschatological salvation as the new Exodus, which is one of the overarching images of the book. But the picture of the lamb standing as though it were slaughtered is also an allusion to Isaiah 53:7. In the context of Deutero-Isaiah's own dominant image of the new Exodus, the picture of the Servant as a lamb led to the slaughter casts the Servant himself in the role of Passover lamb for the new Exodus. Thus, although Revelation is primarily concerned to look forward from the exaltation of Christ to his achievement of the divine lordship at his future coming, still it makes, with its image of the slaughtered lamb on the throne of the universe, essentially the same point as Philippians 2 about the divine identity and rule. The sacrificial death of

Christ belongs to the divine identity as truly as his enthronement and his parousia do, and the divine sovereignty is not fully understood until it is seen to be exercised by the one who witnessed to the truth of God even to the point of death. Only as the slaughtered Lamb is the Christ of Revelation also the first and the last, the Alpha and the Omega.[12] Once again, the inclusion of the earthly Jesus and his death in the identity of God means that the cross reveals who God is.

The humiliation and exaltation of Jesus revealing the divine identity in three examples of the Christian reading of Isaiah 40–55: (3) The Gospel of John

To complete our account of the early Christian reading of Isaiah 40–55 in our three New Testament examples, we must turn again to the Gospel of John. We observed earlier how John places Deutero-Isaiah's great monotheistic self-declaration of God – 'I am he' – on the lips of Jesus in the series of seven absolute 'I am' sayings. We must now see how John relates this making known of God's unique identity in Jesus to the humiliation and passion of Jesus. Approaching this topic via John's interpretation of Deutero-Isaiah will give us a fresh angle on the much debated subject of the Johannine understanding of the cross.

The opening verse of the great Suffering Servant passage in Isaiah (Isa. 52:13) reads:

> Behold, my Servant shall prosper;
> he shall be *exalted* and *lifted up* and shall be very high.

Or in the Septuagint Greek version:

> Behold, my Servant shall understand,
> and shall be exalted *(hupsōthēsetai)* and shall be glorified *(doxasthēsetai)* greatly.

[12] Cf. Bauckham, *The Theology*, 64, 70–71.

Most readers of the Suffering Servant passage, including Paul in Philippians 2 and other New Testament authors, take this first verse to be an anticipatory statement of the exaltation of the Servant which will follow the humiliation, suffering and death that the passage goes on to describe. Isaiah 52:13 announces in advance the exaltation of the Servant which is otherwise only reached at the end of the whole passage (53:12). John, I believe, has interpreted this verse differently. He has taken it as a summary statement of the theme of the whole of the passage it introduces. In other words, the exaltation of the Servant of which this verse speaks is the whole sequence of humiliation, suffering, death and vindication beyond death which chapter 53 describes. The Servant is exalted and glorified in and through his humiliation and suffering. This is the exegetical source for John's theologically profound interpretation of the cross as Jesus' exaltation and glorification.

In the Fourth Gospel there are two principal ways in which Jesus refers to the cross as his coming destiny. Both within the narrative context are enigmatic; both, for the perceptive reader, are theologically potent. Each of them features one of the two verbs with which the Septuagint of Isaiah 52:13 describes the exaltation of the Servant: *hupsoō* (to lift up, to raise high, to exalt) and *doxazō* (to honour, to glorify). We shall consider each in turn.

In place of the passion predictions of the Synoptic Gospels, which state that the Son of Man must suffer, with concrete details of his rejection and death and with probable reference to Isaiah 53 as the prophetic destiny he must fulfil,[13] John has three passion predictions which state that the Son of Man must be 'lifted up' *(hupsoō)*:

> 3:14–15: And just as Moses lifted up *(hupsōsen)* the serpent in the wilderness, so must the Son of Man be lifted up *(hupsōthēnai)*, [15]that whoever believes in him may have eternal life.

[13] Matt. 16:21; 17:23; 20:19; Mark 8:31; 9:31; 10:33–34; Luke 9:22; 18:33.

8:28: So Jesus said, 'When you have lifted up *(hupsōsēte)* the Son of Man, then you will realize that I am he, and that I do nothing on my own, but I speak these things as the Father instructed me.'

12:32–34: 'And I, when I am lifted up *(hupsōthō)* from the earth, will draw all people to myself.' [33]He said this to indicate the kind of death he was to die. [34]The crowd answered him, 'We have heard from the law that the Messiah remains forever. How can you say that the Son of Man must be lifted up *(hupsōthēnai)*? Who is this Son of Man?'

Compared with the passion predications in the Synoptics, in these Johannine sayings the allusion to the Suffering Servant is both more direct and in its peculiar conciseness (the one word 'lifted up') deliberately riddling. Such Johannine enigmas tease the reader into theological enlightenment. In this case, the key is the double meaning of the word. It refers both literally to the crucifixion as a lifting up of Jesus above the earth (as 12:33 makes clear) and figuratively to the same event as Jesus' elevation to the status of divine sovereignty over the cosmos. The cross is already his exaltation. Its physical character, as a literal elevation from the earth, symbolizes its theological character as the decisive movement upwards to heaven as the place of divine sovereignty. The literal elevation, which Jesus' executioners intended as humiliation, an exhibition of his disgrace for all to see, John's readers see, through Deutero-Isaianic eyes, as the event in which Jesus' divine identity is manifested for all to see, thereby drawing all people to himself (12:32). But the full significance in terms of Deutero-Isaianic monotheism we can appreciate only when we observe, as hardly anyone has done, the conjunction in 8:28 of the allusion to Isaiah 52:13 (the lifting up of the Son of Man) with the divine self-declaration, 'I am he,' also from Deutero-Isaiah. This saying is the central one of the three sayings about the lifting up of the Son of Man (3:14–15; 8:28; 12:32–34), and it is also the central saying of the series of seven absolute 'I am' sayings.[14] It deliberately brings the two sets of sayings into theological relationship. *When* Jesus is lifted up,

[14] John 4:26; 6:20; 8:24, 28, 58; 13:19; 18:5–8.

exalted in his humiliation on the cross, *then* the unique divine identity ('I am he') will be revealed for all who can to see. The hope of Deutero-Isaiah, that the one true God will demonstrate his deity to the world, such that all the ends of the earth will turn to him and be saved, is fulfilled when the divine identity is revealed in Jesus' death. These three Son of Man sayings together, not simply repeating but complementing each other, make this comprehensive point: the cross reveals the divine identity in Jesus (8:28), such that all people are drawn to him (12:32) for salvation (3:14–15).

The sayings which refer to Jesus' death as his glorification (two more Son of Man sayings, as well as some others) take up the second key verb from Isaiah 52:13 *(doxazō)*, and make in a different way the same point as those which refer to the lifting up of the Son of Man:

> 12:23: . . . The hour has come for the Son of Man to be glorified *(doxasthē)*.
> 13:31–32: . . . Now the Son of Man has been glorified *(edoxasthē)*, and God has been glorified *(edoxasthē)* in him. If God has been glorified in him, God will also glorify *(doxasei)* him in himself and will glorify him at once.

The verb *(doxazō)* can mean 'to honour' and in that sense points to the same Johannine paradox of the cross. Just as Jesus' humiliation is at the same time his exaltation, so his rejection, his shaming and disgrace in this peculiarly shameful form of death, is paradoxically his honouring by God, in which he also honours God and God also is honoured in him. But John's use of the verb means more than 'honour': it relates to that heavenly splendour (glory) with which other New Testament texts associate the exalted Christ exercising the divine sovereignty. The Fourth Gospel itself gives programmatic prominence to that glory (the heavenly splendour) which is the appearance of God, the manifestation of God's being, when the Prologue claims that 'we have seen his glory, the glory as of a father's only son' (1:14). This glory is the visible manifestation of who God is, reflected in the earthly life of Jesus, a son who is (as it were) the spitting image of his father. It appears in the miracles of Jesus, which reveal his glory, but supremely in the hour of his glorification, when finally the divine identity is manifested on earth as it is in heaven. It is not, of course, that the words 'the Son of man is glorified' can have the literal meaning: 'he manifests the divine glory.' We are dealing rather with a play on words, which links the glorification of the Servant of the Lord (Isa. 52:13) with the revelation of the glory of the Lord, also a Deutero-Isaianic theme:

> Then the glory of the LORD shall be revealed,
> and all flesh shall see it together (Isa. 40:3).

This eschatological manifestation of God's glory – the revelation of who God is – to the world takes place in Jesus' death.

In both sets of sayings – those which refer to the cross as Jesus' lifting up and those which refer to the cross as his glorification – the divine identity is revealed in the paradox of Jesus' death: his humiliation which is in divine reality his exaltation, his shame which is in divine reality his honour. This is a kind of intensification of the theme of Philippians 2:5–11. There the divine identity is revealed in the humiliation and the exaltation as a sequence, in the one who first pours himself out to the ultimate degradation of the cross and is then exalted to the highest position of all. In Philippians the paradox which transforms the meaning of exaltation is that the one who humiliated himself to the utmost is *therefore* exalted to the utmost. But in John the paradox intensifies: Jesus' self-humiliation actually is his exaltation by God. Precisely the same happens with the contrast of lord and servant, which in Philippians 2 is a sequence: the one who is obedient even to the point of dying the death of a slave is therefore exalted to cosmic sovereignty as Lord. Jesus is servant and lord in succession. But in John the whole passion narrative fuses the two themes of lordship and servanthood in simultaneity. Jesus is the king in humility (at the entry into Jerusalem), the king in humiliation (before Pilate and on the cross), and the king in death (his royal burial). Jesus is the lord who serves, who enacts the meaning of his death when he washes the disciples' feet, the menial task exclusive to slaves. His kingship consists in his humiliating service to the point of death. Just as he is exalted in his humiliation and glorified in his disgrace, so also he reigns in being the servant. In this way he reveals who God is. What it means to be God in God's sovereignty and glory appears in the self-humiliation of the one who serves. Once again the Prologue provides the programmatic key, this time in its use of the word 'grace' (1:14, 17). Because God is who God is in his gracious self-giving, God's identity appears in the loving service and self-abnegation to death of his Son. Because God is who God is in his gracious self-giving, God's identity, we can say, is not simply revealed but enacted in the event of salvation for the world which the service and self-humiliation of his Son accomplishes.

The humiliation and exaltation of Jesus revealing the divine identity in three examples of the Christian reading of Isaiah 40–55: Summary

Briefly to recapitulate the testimony of the three New Testament witnesses we have studied to the effect of recognizing the crucified Jesus as belonging to the identity of God: Here God is seen to be God in his radical self-giving, descending to the most abject human condition, and in that human obedience, humiliation, suffering and death, being no less truly God than he is in his cosmic rule and glory on the heavenly throne. It is not that God is manifest in heavenly glory and hidden in the human degradation of the cross. The latter makes known who God is no less than the former does. The divine identity is known in the radical contrast and conjunction of exaltation and humiliation – as the God who is Creator of all things, and no less truly God in the human life of Jesus; as the God who is Sovereign over all things, and no less truly God in Jesus' human obedience and service; as the God of transcendent majesty who is no less truly God in the abject humiliation of the cross. These are not contradictions because God is self-giving love, as much in his creation and rule of all things as in his human incarnation and death. The radical contrast of humiliation and exaltation is precisely the revelation of who God is in his radically self-giving love. He rules only as the one who also serves. He is exalted above all only as the one who is also with the lowest of the low. This is the meaning of the *therefore* of Philippians 2 (*because* Jesus degraded himself to the lowest position *therefore* he was exalted to the highest position). This is the meaning of the slaughtered Lamb's standing as slaughtered on the heavenly throne of God in Revelation 5. This is the meaning of the Johannine paradox that Jesus is exalted and glorified on the cross.

Finally, before we move into the next stage of the argument, it is important to stress that this revelation of the divine identity in the cross does not, for the New Testament writers, mean that the life and death of Jesus are merely an illustration of a general truth about God: that Jesus reveals that God is always like this. In some sense, as we shall shortly see, that was known already to Israel. The story of Jesus is not a mere illustration of the divine identity; Jesus himself and his story are intrinsic to the divine identity. The history of Jesus, his humiliation and his exaltation, is the unique act of God's self-giving, in which he demonstrates his deity to the world by accomplishing salvation for the world. In the words of the Johannine prologue, through Jesus Christ grace and truth *happened* – the divine self-giving occurred in full reality – and in this way the glory of the God whom no one has ever seen was revealed (John 1:14–18). In this act of self-giving God is most truly himself and defines himself for the world.

God crucified and the God of Israel: novelty and consistency

Now we turn to the stage of our argument in which we must relate this result to our starting point, in other words, to the identity of the God of Israel revealed in the Hebrew scriptures. If Jesus reveals who God is, if God's identity is as God crucified, how does this revelation relate to the identity of the God of Israel? Is this the same God? Is his identity in Jesus consistent with his identity in the Old Testament revelation?

Is the revelation of his identity in Jesus only the universal revelation, to the world, of the divine identity already fully known to Israel? Or is his identity more fully known in Jesus?

To answer such questions, we must revert to my initial account, in chapter 1, of the way biblical and post-biblical Israel understood the identity of Israel's God. From that account I isolated two of the key features of the divine identity, and pursued the rest of my argument in the first two chapters in terms of these two features, which were the creative and sovereign activity of God. The point of isolating these two features was that it was on God as the Creator of all things and God as the sovereign Ruler of all things that Jewish understanding of the uniqueness of the one God focused. These are the two features of the divine identity which serve most clearly to distinguish God from all other reality and to identify God as the unique one, who alone relates to all other things as their Creator and Sovereign. These features therefore also served to make unequivocally clear the New Testament writers' inclusion of Jesus in the unique divine identity. However, while these two features serve most clearly to distinguish God from all other reality, they by no means sufficiently characterize God's relationship to his creation and by no means sufficiently identify God as he was known in his self-revelation to Israel. Israel had much else to say about the divine identity. In this connexion, in chapter 1, I made two main points, both of which concern God's relationship to his covenant people. First, God is identified by his acts in Israel's history, especially in the Exodus. Secondly, God is known from his character description given to Moses: 'merciful and gracious, slow to anger, and abounding in steadfast love and faithfulness' (Exod 34:6). The acts of God in Israel's history and the character description of God together identify God as the one who acts graciously towards his people. Together they serve for Israel to define who God is.

However, the God so identified was expected, on the basis of this very identity, to act again in the future, in a way consistent with his already known identity. Thus Deutero-Isaiah, in a way especially important for the early Christians, expects a new Exodus event, on the model of the first but far transcending the first Exodus. God will demonstrate his deity to Israel and to the ends of the earth, and will act for the salvation not only of Israel but of all peoples. It is no accident that Deutero-Isaiah's God is both the covenant God of the Exodus and also the Creator and Ruler of all things. In the eschatological Exodus he will prove to be the God of all peoples, Sovereign and Saviour of all, in a way consistent with his identity as the gracious God of his people Israel. His uniqueness as Creator and Ruler of all will be universally acknowledged when he acts graciously for the salvation of Israel and the world.

It follows that, for those – the early Christians – who have experienced this new Exodus, a new narrative of God's acts becomes definitive of his identity. Just as Israel identified God as the God who brought Israel out of Egypt and by telling the story of God's history with Israel, so the New Testament identifies God as the God of Jesus Christ and by telling the story of Jesus as the story of the salvation of the world. The new story is consistent with the already known identity of the God of Israel, but new as the way he now identifies himself finally and universally, the Creator and Ruler of all who in Jesus Christ has become the gracious saviour of all. So far the novelty is what could be expected of the God known to Israel. But is there not something more radically novel because unexpected and surprising? When early Christians included Jesus himself, a human being, humiliated and exalted, in the identity of God; when they told the story of Jesus, whether in summary form in Philippians 2:5–11 or in extended detail in the Fourth Gospel, as the story of God's own human obedience, humility, degradation and death, were they not saying something radically new about the identity of God? If so we must press the question of its consistency with the known identity of the God of Israel. An important point to make in this connexion is that the identity of the God of Israel does not exclude the unexpected and surprising. Quite the contrary, this God's freedom as God requires his freedom from all human expectations, even those based on his revealed identity. He may act in new and surprising ways, in which he proves to be the same God, consistent with his known identity, but in unexpected ways. He is both free and faithful. He is not capricious but nor is he predictable. He may be trusted to be consistent with himself, but he may surprise in the ways he proves consistent with himself. The consistency can only be appreciated with hindsight.

The question then is how the early Christians found the consistency in the novelty. If God crucified introduces radical novelty into the identity of God, wherein lies the consistency of identity? The first point to make is simply to reiterate what we established earlier in this book, that Jewish monotheism did not characterize the uniqueness of God in such a way as to make the early Christian inclusion of Jesus in the unique identity of God inconceivable. Those scholars, including many New Testament scholars, who assume that no Jewish monotheist could have accepted divine Christology, including Jesus in the divine identity, without abandoning Jewish monotheism have not understood Jewish monotheism. However, this – so to speak – negative consistency was clearly not sufficient for the early Christians. What is so impressive in the material we have studied is the way they developed their fresh understanding of the christological identity of God *through* creative exegesis of the Hebrew scriptures. To illustrate this (which could certainly also have been illustrated in other ways) I have focused on their exegesis of Deutero-Isaiah. Precisely at the points where they appreciate most fully the new identity of God in Jesus they are engaged in exegesis, in the process of bringing the texts of the Hebrew scriptures and the history of Jesus into mutually interpretative interplay. We misunderstand this process if we see it as an attempt, by reading Christology back into the texts, to pretend that actually nothing at all was unexpected. The first Christians knew better than we do that some of the key insights they found in Deutero-Isaiah had not been seen in Deutero-Isaiah before. But the work of creative exegesis enabled them to find consistency in the novelty. They appreciate the most radically new precisely in the process of understanding its continuity with the already revealed. With deliberate hindsight they understand the identity of the God of Israel afresh in the light of his new identity as the God of Jesus Christ. They find him to be one and the same God, not in ways which could have been predicted, but in ways which in this light now come to light.

So I will make three further main points about this question of consistency and novelty in the identity of God. First, we return to the contrast in Philippians 2 between high and low status, exaltation and humiliation, honour and shame. This contrast seems to me the point at which the inclusion of the human life and shameful death of Jesus in the identity of God must have seemed, for Second Temple Judaism's understanding of God, most remarkable. The image of God the sovereign Ruler on his majestic throne high above all the heavens was so dominant in Second Temple Judaism that the notion of divine self-degradation to the lowest human status could easily have seemed quite inconceivable. This issue of divine and human status would be the stumbling-block, rather than later problems which the Christian doctrine of incarnation was to encounter subsequently: the unitary nature of a God who cannot be internally differentiated, or definitions of divine and human nature which present them as incompatible. Such problems are barely visible in the New Testament, but the contrast of divine height and human lowliness, sovereign exaltation and servile degradation is a preoccupation. Yet, whatever the impression some post-biblical Jewish literature may give, the identity of the God of Israel already includes, in some sense, his lowliness as well as his exaltation. Isaiah 57:15, a text we have already encountered in relation to Philippians 2:5–11, reads:

> . . . thus says the exalted and lofty One
> who inhabits eternity, whose name is Holy:
> 'I dwell in the high and holy place,
> *and also* with those who are crushed and lowly in spirit . . .'

The God of Israel, indeed, is characteristically the God of the lowly and the humiliated, the God who hears the cry of the oppressed, the God who raises the poor from the dust, the God who from his throne on high identifies with those in the depths, the God who exercises his sovereignty on high in solidarity with those of lowest status here below. In drawing on the narrative of the Servant of the Lord, humiliated and exalted, from Isaiah 53, Paul in Philippians 2:5–11 thereby evokes this characteristic of the identity of the God of Israel. The radical novelty in Philippians 2 lies in the way in which God in Jesus Christ dwells in the depths, not only with but *as* the lowest of the low. God's characteristic exaltation of the lowest becomes a pattern in which he participates himself. This could not have been expected, but nor is it uncharacteristic. It is novel but appropriate to the identity of the God of Israel.

Secondly, the way the Prologue to John relates the revelation of God in the incarnation to the identity of the God of Israel is instructive. The last verses of the Prologue (John 1:14–18) claim that God, who has never been seen by human eyes, has been revealed in the human life of Jesus Christ, who reflects his Father's glory and is full of grace and truth. All these terms allude to the story of God's revelation of himself to Moses in Exodus 33–34, in which the central Old Testament character description of God occurs. There Moses asks to see God's glory (33:18), is told that he cannot see God's face, but as God covers Moses' eyes and passes by, he hears God proclaim his name and his character: 'YHWH, YHWH, a God merciful and gracious, slow to anger, and abounding in steadfast love and faithfulness' (Exod 34:6) – or in John's translation 'full of grace and truth' (John 1:14).[15] Moses could only hear God's word proclaiming *that* God is full of grace and truth. He could not see God's glory. But in the Word made flesh, God's glory was seen in human form, and grace and truth (according to John 1:17) happened or came about *(egeneto)*. Thus God's gracious love, central to the identity of the God of Israel, now takes the radically new form of a *human life* in which the divine self-giving happens. This could not have been expected, but nor is it uncharacteristic. It is novel but appropriate to the identity of the God of Israel.

Thirdly, the point which may well seem to us most startlingly novel about the new identity of God in Jesus is one which I have deliberately not made explicit until now: that the

---

[15] Cf. A. T. Hanson, *Grace and Truth* (London: SPCK, 1975) chapter 1.

inclusion of Jesus in the identity of God means the inclusion in God of the interpersonal relationship between Jesus and his Father. No longer can the divine identity be purely and simply portrayed by analogy with a single human subject. And since the portrayal of God in the Hebrew Bible does, to a large extent, employ the analogy of a human agent, this might seem such a radical innovation as to throw doubt on the consistency of the divine identity. But if we think so we may be attributing to the biblical writers too unsubtly anthropomorphic ways of thinking. While human identity may be the common analogy for thinking about the divine identity, the God of Israel clearly transcends the categories of human identity. The categories are used in awareness that God transcends them. In God's unique relationship to the rest of reality as Creator of all things and sovereign Ruler of all things, the human analogies, indispensable as they are, clearly point to a divine identity transcendently other than human personhood. Nothing in the Second Temple Jewish understanding of divine identity contradicts the possibility of interpersonal relationship within the divine identity, but on the other hand there is little, if anything, that anticipates it.

The novelty of divine identity revealed as intra-divine relationship is, in my view, strikingly acknowledged in one New Testament text in the way most appropriate to the biblical tradition of understanding the divine identity. In this text God acquires a new name which identifies him in this newly revealed form of his identity. In order to appreciate this text, it may help first to go back to the occasion in the Old Testament narrative on which God discloses his name, YHWH, by which he had not previously been known. To Moses at the burning bush in Exodus 3 God identifies himself as the God of the patriarchs, the God of Abraham, Isaac and Jacob (3:6), but this identity is not sufficient for the events in which he is to bring Israel out of Egypt and make them his people. The disclosure of the name by which his people are now to know him is required for his new identity, in which his old identity as the God of the patriarchs is by no means repudiated but is certainly surpassed. Since the patriarchal stories have appropriately been called 'the Old Testament of the Old Testament,'[16] the transition from the God of the patriarchs to YHWH the God of Israel is a kind of precedent for the transition from the latter to the God of Jesus Christ. Once again a new name identifies the newly disclosed identity, although this clearly occurs only in one New Testament text: Matthew 28:19.

Though unique, this text is a significant one and deserves attention to its context. To a Gospel in which God has, of course, repeatedly been identified with the God of Israel, but in which the inclusion of Jesus in this divine identity has also repeatedly been indicated,[17] the last five verses form a climax. The risen Jesus receives worship and declares his exaltation to exercise of the divine sovereignty over all things (Matt. 28:18: 'all authority in heaven and on earth'). His inclusion in the divine identity is now unequivocal. The scene is a Gospel equivalent to the last part of the christological passage in Philippians 2:5–11. But whereas in that passage it is the Old Testament divine name, YHWH, that the exalted Christ receives, here the disciples are to baptize 'in the name of the Father and of the Son and of the Holy Spirit' (verse 19). The formula, as in the phrase 'calling on the name of the Lord' which New Testament usage takes up from the Old with reference to baptism and profession of Christian faith, requires precisely a divine name. 'The Father, the Son and the Holy Spirit' names the newly disclosed identity of God, revealed in the story of Jesus the Gospel has told.

In conclusion, therefore, to this discussion of consistency and novelty in the New Testament revelation of the identity of God, we can say that in Christ God both demonstrates his deity to the world as the same unique God his people Israel had always known, and also, in doing so, identifies himself afresh. As the God who includes the humiliated and the exalted Jesus in his identity he is the Father, the Son and the Holy

---

16 R. W. Moberly, *The Old Testament of the Old Testament* (OBT; Minneapolis: Fortress, 1992).

17 Cf. D. D. Kupp, *Matthew's Emmanuel: Divine Presence and God's People in the First Gospel* (SNTSMS 90; Cambridge: Cambridge University Press, 1996).

Spirit, that is, the Father of Jesus Christ, Jesus Christ the Son, and the Spirit of the Father given to the Son.

Evaluating later christological–theological developments

This all-too-brief concluding section will indicate what the implications of my argument about New Testament Christology would be for evaluating later theological developments, in the patristic period and later. It may be helpful here to reiterate for the last time the two key points I have argued about the relationship between monotheism and Christology in the New Testament: (1) New Testament writers clearly and deliberately include Jesus in the unique identity of the God of Israel; (2) The inclusion of the human life and shameful death, as well as the exaltation of Jesus, in the divine identity reveals the divine identity – who God is – in a new way.

If we look beyond the New Testament, this interpretation of New Testament Christology makes possible a fresh evaluation of the continuity between the New Testament and the patristic development of dogma, in particular the achievement of Nicene orthodoxy in the fourth century. Broadly speaking, there seem to be two dominant ways of interpreting the development from New Testament Christology to the Council of Nicaea and beyond. The first sees the New Testament as containing in embryonic form the source of the development which culminated in the Nicene theology of the fourth century. In other words, New Testament Christology is moving in the direction of recognizing Jesus Christ as truly and fully God, but it was left to the theologians of the fourth century to bring such fully divine Christology to full expression and to find adequate ways of stating it within the context of a trinitarian doctrine of God. Against this first interpretation, my argument has been that, once we understand Jewish monotheism properly, we can see that the New Testament writers are already, in a deliberate and sophisticated way, expressing a fully divine Christology by including Jesus in the unique identity of God as defined by Second Temple Judaism. Once we recognize the theological categories with which they are working, it is clear that there is nothing embryonic or tentative about this. In its own terms, it is an adequate expression of a fully divine Christology. It is, as I have called it, a Christology of divine identity. The developmental model, according to which the New Testament sets a christological direction only completed in the fourth century, is therefore seriously flawed.

The second way of interpreting the evidence supposes that a Christology which attributed true divinity to Jesus could not have originated within a context of Jewish monotheism. On this view divine Christology is the result of a transition from Jewish to Hellenistic religious and subsequently Hellenistic philosophical categories. Nicaea represents the triumph of Greek philosophy in Christian doctrine. This way of reading the history seems to me to be virtually the opposite of the truth. In other words, it was actually not Jewish but Greek philosophical categories which made it difficult to attribute true and full divinity to Jesus. A Jewish understanding of divine identity was open to the inclusion of Jesus in the divine identity. But Greek philosophical – Platonic – definitions of divine substance or nature and Platonic understanding of the relationship of God to the world made it extremely difficult to see Jesus as more than a semi-divine being, neither truly God nor truly human. In the context of the Arian controversies, Nicene theology was essentially an attempt to resist the implications of Greek philosophical understandings of divinity and to re-appropriate in a new conceptual context the New Testament's inclusion of Jesus in the unique divine identity.

The conceptual shift from Jewish to Greek categories was from categories focused on divine identity – who God is – to categories focused on divine being or nature – what God is. The credal slogan of Nicene theology – the *homoousion* (that Christ is of the same substance as the Father) – may look initially like a complete capitulation to Greek categories. But the impression is different when we understand its function within the trinitarian and narrative context it has in, for example, the Nicene and Niceno-Constantinopolitan Creeds. This context identifies God as Father, Son and Holy Spirit, and identifies God from the narrative of the history of Jesus. The *homoousion* in this context functions to ensure that this divine identity is truly the identity of the one and only God. In its own way it expresses the christological monotheism of the New Testament.

However, if the patristic development of dogma secured for a new conceptual context the New Testament's inclusion of Jesus in the unique divine identity, the Fathers were much less successful in appropriating the second key feature of New Testament Christology to which I have drawn attention: the revelation of the divine identity in the human life of Jesus and his cross. Here the shift to categories of divine nature and the Platonic definition of divine nature which the fathers took for granted proved serious impediments to anything more than a formal inclusion of human humiliation, suffering and death in the identity of God. That God was crucified is indeed a patristic formulation, but the Fathers largely resisted its implications for the doctrine of God. Adequate theological appropriation of the deepest insights of New Testament Christology, such as we have observed in Philippians 2:5–11 and the Fourth Gospel, was not to occur until Martin Luther, Karl Barth and more recent theologies of the cross.[18]

---

[18] See R. Bauckham, *Moltmann: Messianic Theology in the Making* (Basingstoke: Marshall Pickering, 1987) 65–72; idem, 'Cross, Theology of the', in S. B. Ferguson and D. F. Wright ed., *New Dictionary of Theology* (Leicester: Inter-Varsity Press, 1988) 181–183; idem, 'Jesus the Revelation of God', in P. Avis ed., *Divine Revelation* (London: Darton, Longman & Todd; Grand Rapids: Eerdmans, 1997) 182–187; W. von Loewenich, *Luther's Theology of the Cross* (tr. H. J. A. Bouman; Belfast: Christian Journals, 1976); A. E. McGrath, *Luther's Theology of the Cross* (Oxford: Blackwell, 1985); D. K. P. Ngien, *The Suffering of God According to Martin Luther's 'Theologia Crucis'* (Bern/New York: Peter Lang, 1995); J. Moltmann, *The Crucified God* (tr. R. A. Wilson and J. Bowden; London: SCM, 1974); E. Jüngel, *God as the Mystery of the World* (tr. D. L. Guder; Edinburgh: T. & T. Clark, 1983).